DR. JOHN SPENCER

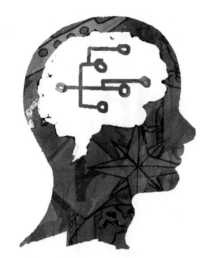

THE **A.I.**

ROADMAP

HUMAN LEARNING IN THE AGE
OF SMART MACHINES

The A.I. Roadmap: Human Learning in the Age of Smart Machines

BLEND

Blend Education Publishing
PO Boz 5953
Salem, OR 97304

ISBN: 978-1-7341726-4-5

TABLE OF CONTENTS

PART ONE

HOW WILL EDUCATORS RESPOND TO ARTIFICIAL INTELLIGENCE?

The A.I. Roadmap

CHAPTER 1
THE A.I. REVOLUTION IS ALREADY HERE

Three years ago, I stood in a university innovation lab, surrounded by high-tech gadgetry. But in this moment, I wasn't focused on the state-of-the-art robots with their hydraulic limbs or the latest Virtual Reality simulation. Instead, I stared at an ordinary flat screen monitor.

The professor leaned forward and said, "Ready to see something mind-blowing?"

"Yes, please," I answered.

All at once, a student work sample appeared. This was the opposite of mind-blowing. It was Calculus homework. I read the student's question about fluid flow and heat transfer and nodded as if I understood the equation. However, this was an aspect of Calculus I either never learned or never understood. Either way, I could only vaguely grasp what was going on.

The professor clicked a button. Two additional writing samples appeared – each offering their own form of feedback for the student. Still not mind-blowing in the least.

"Which one is human-generated?" he asked.

I read through both responses and shook my head.

He cleared his throat and asked, "Can you determine which of these feedback samples was generated via machine learning?"

I studied both answers again, looking for clues in the syntax. I tried to find the humanity within the language. Perhaps some idioms or casual language to clue me in to the human element. But I couldn't tell the difference. Both options were clear and concise with just a touch of colloquial friendliness. I shook my head and studied the writing yet again, but the difference was indistinguishable.

"Are they both the A.I.?" I asked.

"It's easy to think that. The grad student is an engineer, and we tend to be a little robotic when giving feedback," he answered.

"I can't tell the difference between them," I confessed.

"The correct answer is B," he said.

I stood in the lab baffled by the progression of machine learning. This wasn't merely "close enough." This was it. Artificial Intelligence had finally arrived, and I had officially failed the Turing Test.[1] I couldn't tell whether I was interacting with a human or a machine.

He then continued, "Don't feel bad. The students can't tell the difference either. To them, it's just a chat with an expert."

"So, you didn't tell the students which one was the A.I.?" I asked.

"That's part of the experimental study," he responded. "We want to see how students respond to A.I."

My head swirled with questions of the Turing Test and the Eliza Effect and the notion of singularity (ideas we'll explore later). I thought about deep fakes and the future of humanity. I'm pretty sure an image from *Blade Runner* popped into my head and maybe a scene of Data from *Star Trek TNG*.

But more than anything else, I had the nagging question, "Will A.I. replace me?" After all, I had spent hours that week assessing student work. Yet this bot could provide targeted feedback in seconds. And it was good. Really good.

For the rest of the day, I distracted myself with the workshop I led on student voice and choice. I told stories, shared examples, and enjoyed the laughter we had as a group. But as I walked away from the innovation lab and headed into the early autumn evening, I couldn't shake the image of the A.I. feedback.

Would A.I. replace assessment or merely amplify it and transform it? Maybe I could spend less time writing out feedback and more time doing one-on-one conferences with that human, dynamic element. Maybe students would initiate the feedback using an A.I. chatbot but then meet with me during office hours for a second opinion. Or maybe my role as a professor would change entirely. Perhaps I would review the A.I. feedback to make sure it's on target. Maybe I would use it as another tool – not unlike a rubric.

WOULD A.I. REPLACE ME?

Or maybe not. Perhaps the entire role of an educator would change. Maybe I would shift toward being more of a course architect and designer. The university would save money by providing a cheaper college experience with even less of a human element and the students wouldn't even know the difference. A human professor would be a luxury rather than a necessity. As I left campus and began exploring the city, I couldn't shake the uneasiness I felt about machine learning and what it meant for our future.

THE A.I. REVOLUTION IS ALREADY HERE

Fast forward five years. Suddenly, we are having a cultural moment where we are recognizing the power of Artificial Intelligence. It's been a slow build. Auto-correct here. Grammarly suggestion there. An auto-fill option in G-mail and in Google Searches. A small chat at the bottom left-hand corner with A.I. who will help you get that refund on the flight you purchased from Expedia. But it always felt small and in the margins. Then ChatGPT came along and suddenly we are left asking, "What does this mean for the future of work? What does mean for teaching and learning?" [2]

The revolution is happening at a breakneck speed. In the first week alone, ChatGPT surpassed a million users.[3] To put that in perspective, it took Instagram two years to reach that benchmark. By January, the A.I. platform had surpassed 100 million users.[4]

I played around with it for hours in the first day it came out; mostly in goofy ways, like turning the Gettysburg Address into a limerick or retelling a Taylor Swift song in the style of J.R.R. Tolkien. But then I shifted toward a more practical mode. I used it to come up with a new workout plan.[5] I used it to make a playlist of nostalgic songs for middle aged suburban parents at a barbecue. It nailed the Weezer recommendations.

But I also explored how well it did in answering the kinds of questions I once asked my middle school students. I started with a writing prompt for an eighth-grade social studies class. Could the A.I. compare 19th century imperialism to 21st century globalization? Absolutely. The answer was creative and exhibited strong critical thinking. I added a parameter. "Explain it to someone who is 14." This was the answer:

> Imperialism and globalization are similar in that they both involve the expansion of a country's power and influence over other countries. However, there are some key differences between the two.
>
> 19th century imperialism was a form of aggressive expansionism in which powerful countries, such as Britain, France, and Germany, used their military and economic might to conquer and control other nations. This often involved the exploitation of natural resources and the exploitation of local people.
>
> On the other hand, 21st century globalization is a more complex and interconnected process in which countries and businesses around the world are increasingly linked through trade, technology, and other forms of exchange. Globalization has brought many benefits, such as increased economic growth and access to new markets, but it has also sparked debates about inequality and the impact on local cultures.
>
> In summary, imperialism was a one-sided process in which powerful countries imposed their will on others, while globalization is a more complex and interconnected process that involves both cooperation and competition between countries.

This read like an essay written by a thirteen-year-old student. I took a deep breath. No big deal. I could always tell the writing style of my students. But then I gave the chatbot examples of my own writing and asked it to mimic my style. While it wasn't perfect, it was surprisingly solid.

Was this the future of writing?

As an avid illustrator, I decided to play around with the A.I. picture generators. I used an app that created a picture of me as a Viking from the past. I wasn't sure if they would go with historical Viking or member of the Midwestern football team that still hasn't won a Super Bowl in its long franchise history. The A.I. went historical. This was the result.

It doesn't capture the forehead wrinkles or the bags under my eyes (or as I like to call them, "visual evidence of my years as a middle school teacher"). But still, I'm surprised by how well the A.I. captures my facial features.

Again, I am wondering about what this means for our future. I have always felt like creativity — and visual creativity in particular — was a distinctly human endeavor. However, A.I. did a fantastic job with the portrait in a matter of seconds.

I've been following A.I. closely for over a decade. I experienced the challenges brought on by my middle school students using A.I. to solve math problems. I've paid attention to some of the applications in engineering and wondered what this might mean in the future. But I always viewed this as the distant future. Something far off. Some day.

But that "some day?" It's here. That distant future? It's right now. Our students are already using generative A.I.

There are times when I feel excited about its potential strengths and moments when I am terrified of its drawbacks. But more than anything, I am trying to understand how A.I. works and how it might change human systems. As I talk to teachers around the globe, I notice many of the same emotions that I feel.

EXCITED BY THE
POSSIBILITIES

SCARED ABOUT
THE FUTURE

CONFUSED BY
HOW AI WORKS

CURIOUS ABOUT
HOW TO USE AI

ANGRY ABOUT THE
CHANGES AI BRINGS ON

WILL A.I. BE HELPFUL OR HARMFUL?

When I first began interviewing A.I. experts, I imagined the worst-case scenario. Robot overlords. Technology gone rogue. A.I. growing too smart and sentient and deciding to launch nuclear weapons. However, as these computer scientists described how A.I. actually functions, I realized that most of my fears were based on science fiction rather than science fact.

Many A.I. proponents have pointed out how machine learning could help with research and development. Efficient grid systems could improve supply chains and thus reduce carbon emissions. If food waste plummets, the whole planet benefits. Moreover, A.I. is one aspect of why we got the COVID vaccine so quickly.[6] Proponents of A.I. point to a future where we might find cures for diseases, reduce medical malpractice, and create safer driving conditions. A.I. is already reducing human error. The use of autopilot on aircrafts has reduced the number of fatal crashes despite having more planes in the sky.

On a more mundane level, A.I. is promising in its ability to automate boring tasks. You might spend more time making videos but less time with the monotony of video editing. As an educator, you might use it to do monotonous tasks (like testing for reading fluency) so you can focus more of your energy on building a positive classroom culture.

But there's also potential for significant harm. While A.I. might help with research and development, the speed and efficiency might just reduce the number of actual jobs required to do the task. Even if A.I. creates a set of new jobs, this job displacement will create massive disruptions in the upcoming decades. A.I.-fueled deepfakes will grow more realistic, leading to huge issues of misinformation. Even with guardrails intact, we can't predict how this technology might go rogue.[7] A.I. will have unintended consequences.

Recently, prominent computer scientists, ethicists, and philosophers have called for a pause on A.I. development.[8] This isn't an anti-A.I. stance so much as a "let's slow down and see what it means to use it wisely" approach. In *A Human's Guide to Machine Intelligence*, Kartik Hosanagar argues that we need to develop an Algorithmic Bill of Rights.[9]

I am deeply concerned about the role of A.I. in misinformation. Therefore, I devote an entire chapter to the topic of information literacy and what it means on a social level (with democracy) and an individual level (with issues like catfishing). I'm also concerned about job displacement. I don't know if A.I. will replace more jobs than it creates but I know the disruption will be hard on certain communities. For this reason, we explore the changes that might occur in the realms of creativity, project-based learning, and CTE programs.

However, I have been impressed by the potential of A.I. to solve complex human problems. I get excited about how it might be used in an ethical way to improve our world. In this book, we'll focus on a human-centered approach to A.I. in learning. We'll explore some of the possibilities for making learning more accessible, more relevant, and more human.

Ultimately, I'm not sure if A.I. is inherently harmful or helpful so much as it is powerful. And with anything this powerful, there will be significant tradeoffs for our society. These tradeoffs are going to impact our classrooms in ways that we cannot even predict. Therefore, we need a roadmap.

THE NEED FOR A ROADMAP

The hardest part of this A.I. Revolution is the sheer unpredictability of machine learning. I want a clear picture of the future. Let me know exactly what A.I. will look like in the next decade and I can design a personal plan for how I will respond. But that's not how disruptive technology works. We can't predict precisely how machine learning will change the way we think and learn.

The truth is we don't know how A.I. will change learning, thinking, and education in the upcoming decade (an idea we'll explore in-depth in Chapter 5). This why I can't offer a step-by-step blueprint for how we should approach A.I. moving forward. I can't craft an instruction manual for how we should re-imagine learning.

But what I can offer is a roadmap. In this map, we explore the newly emerging terrain of machine learning in education.

To be clear, I'm not the expert guide. I don't have a degree in computer science or engineering. I've never designed an A.I. system. I'm an educator. I started out as a middle school teacher and now I'm a full-time professor. For the last five years, I've been an explorer asking the experts some of the big questions I've been wrestling with regarding how A.I. will change the learning environment for our classrooms.

While my focus area as a professor is educational technology, I'm not even that much of a techie. Just two minutes ago, I accidentally changed my lock screen on my phone and had to ask my daughter how to fix it. I try to stay up to date but you won't see me use a term like "app smashing" at any of the technology conferences I attend.

Instead, I'm interested in what student-centered learning looks like in an unpredictable world. I explore what it means to engage in authentic projects in a context that's constantly changing. For years, I have wrestled with the question, "What does human learning look like in a world of smart machines?"

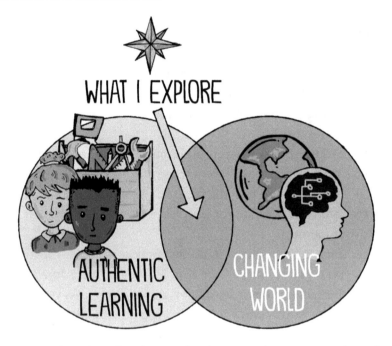

For nearly a decade, I have talked to countless experts about how A.I. works and what that might mean for our schools. I have interviewed computer scientists, engineers, curriculum designers, classroom teachers, Big Data experts, policy wonks, and K-12 leaders with the hope of getting a bigger picture of what's emerging with A.I. and learning. I have read scholarly journals and popular articles and any book I could get my hands on to make sense out of A.I.

In this book, I will take you on a journey as a co-traveler. We start out by asking, "What is A.I. and how is this newer, generative A.I., different from the A.I. we've already been using?" Next, we explore two dead ends we want to avoid as we approach A.I. in education.

From there, we look out at the horizon and recognize that we don't know entirely what lies ahead.

As we shift to Part 2, we will examine what it means to navigate the changing definition of creativity. We'll look at the need for new tools and mindsets as students explore the changing media and information terrain. We will navigate what it means to use A.I. wisely in project-based learning and how we might take a human-centered approach to personalized learning, assessment, and student supports.

In Part 3, we will head into more specific trails as we explore the ways A.I. is transforming the terrain of various subjects and disciplines. We will end this journey with the big question, "How will A.I. change my role as a teacher?"

This roadmap offers multiple trails that crisscross all around. Every teacher is going to take a different route as they navigate a changing world. I encourage you to treat this book as a map. If there are sections that aren't as relevant for you, feel free to skip a chapter. After all, it's your journey!

The scary thing is there is no instruction manual. The exciting thing is you'll get to forge your own journey moving forward. The beautiful thing is you won't be on this journey alone. As you collaborate with other educators, you'll gain insights into what it means to use A.I. wisely.

Let the journey begin!

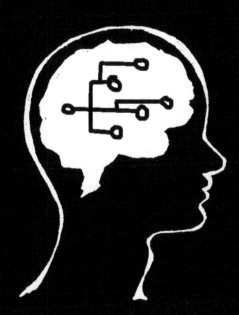

CHAPTER 2

WHAT DO WE MEAN BY ARTIFICIAL INTELLIGENCE?

Before we get started with this chapter, I want to define a few technical A.I. terms you might see.

Algorithm: a set of instructions that a computer can follow to solve a problem or perform a task. It's like a recipe or a set of directions that tells the machine what steps to take.

Artificial Intelligence (A.I.): the use of advanced algorithms to perform tasks that usually require human intelligence, such as problem-solving, learning, and perception.

Deep Learning: a subset of machine learning that uses neural networks to analyze complex data and make predictions or decisions.

Generative A.I.: a type of A.I. that can create original content, such as images, music, or text, similar to what humans can produce.

Machine Learning: a method of training machines to make decisions or predictions based on data, without being explicitly programmed to do so.

Natural Language Processing: a branch of A.I. that focuses on enabling computers to understand, interpret, and generate human language. Programs like ChatGPT have been trained on a massive dataset and use a combination of deep learning and statistical techniques to generate responses to user inputs that are similar in style and tone to human-generated text.

Neural Networks: a type of machine learning algorithm that uses layers of interconnected nodes, similar to neurons in the human brain, to process and analyze information.

Miguel rolls over and looks at the recommended players for his Fantasy Football team. Not bad. An alert pops up with the latest news. The stock market is in decline, but he has no idea what that means for his retirement account. Apparently, they have robot investors. He's not entirely sure how it works but there's a projection of how much he'll likely have when he's retired, and he hopes that's enough to have a boat.

Emily snags her phone and texts her mom. "Hope the appointment goes well."

"Thank you. See you at Christmas. I can't believe it will be the first time since the panda medic."

A split second later her mom writes, "You know I meant pandemic, right? This doggone voice to text."

"I know," Emily answers.

"I got an alert that plane tickets are the lowest they're going to be. You should buy them now," her mom texts.

"Thanks, mom," she answers before rolling out of bed and putting on the matching pajamas she and Miguel will be wearing for their Fun Friday Spirit Day. Seems like half the days in elementary school require a special theme of some sort. Yesterday was 80's day. Miguel thought it would be funny to dress like an octogenarian, but nobody understood the joke. Today they are wearing the matching PJs they bought on impulse after they got the same advertisement on Instagram and ended up buying each other a monthly pajama subscription as an anniversary present.

Miguel turns to the smart thermostat. It already knows to ramp up the heat when they get out of bed but he doublechecks it just in case.

"Wild," he mutters to himself as Emily pours herself a cup of coffee.

"I thought we were getting coffee," Miguel says.

"This is my pre-coffee coffee. Fridays are . . . well . . . Friday and third graders are . . . well . . . third graders," she answers.

"Got it," he nods.

"I'm going to save my cold brew for the afternoon," she says. In less than a minute, she downs her entire mug.

"Kitchen dance party?" Miguel asks.

Emily nods. This has been a Friday morning tradition since they first met years ago on a dating app. Emily tells the smart speaker to turn on the music.

Miguel opens their curated pick-me-up playlist designed specifically by the streaming service to match their tastes. The Friday morning kitchen dance party commences.

It isn't pretty but it is fun – and fun beats pretty any time you have a kitchen dance party.

Once out of breath, Emily sends a social media message to her colleague. Supplies haven't arrived for their Maker Monday activity, so she might have to stop by the store this weekend. Her friend mentions a new series she's been binge-watching that showed up in her recommended feed. It's about a group of sisters that try to murder their brother-in-law but keep failing at it.

Miguel glances at his smartwatch. He's already ahead of schedule in movement and calories burned.

An alert pops up as his wrist vibrates.

"Did you hear about how unhinged the School Board meeting got last night?" Miguel's friend texts.

"Wow," he answers using the voice-to-text app.

"I wouldn't want to be a librarian right now," his friend replies. His friend wants a big conversation about book banning. Miguel just wants a cup of coffee.

Miguel glances at the weather app in the smart fridge and decides on a coat instead of a sweatshirt over his pajamas. He pops open the app for the coffee store and clicks on the suggested order. A calorie-tracking app offers a quick alert about his weekly progress. Better ditch the blueberry muffin. He modifies the coffee order and grabs his keys.

"I'll get our coffee and we'll carpool together?" he asks.

"Is it carpooling if you're married?" she asks.

"I think so. It's eco-friendly, either way. So, I think we get imaginary green points for this."

They hug and he heads out the door. Emily stresses about the upcoming district benchmark tests and the predictive analytics of the "bubble kids" who might not pass. Miguel heads out to the car.

It's less than twenty minutes into the day and yet Emily and Miguel are already immersed in the world of A.I. It fuels the facial recognition that allows them to open their phones instantaneously. It runs their thermostat and appliances as they get out of bed.

When Emily interacts with her mom, A.I. is silently present in the voice-to-text and autocorrect features they both use. On a more serious note, A.I. will catch an abnormality at her mother's appointment that leads to an early detection of cancer and saves her mom's life.

As they think about travel, A.I. is pervasive, from the prices to the recommendations to the booking system to the autopilot to the customer service interactions to the fraud detection software that will shut down their credit card when they decide to buy everyone a round of drinks in Fargo and then later in the car sharing app that allows them to get home safely after they both had a few too many adult beverages that very same night.

A.I. sets the recommendations of products to buy and decides the songs they will dance to in the kitchen, as well as the recommendation to avoid playing the San Francisco 49ers defense in Fantasy Football because of the complex algorithm determining just how poorly the Niners fare against the read-option offense.

In fact, Artificial Intelligence fueled the dating app that led the couple to one another in the first place. On a more mundane level, it predicts the weather, which today means a high likelihood of needing a coat to cover light pajamas for the final day of Spirit Week. But it also chooses their stocks and sets up their investment portfolio.

The A.I. creates a customized challenge to earn bonus points for Miguel in the coffee store app. A.I. predicts what Miguel will order. But it also fuels the employee system that estimates how long it will take for the order to be ready. It sets the data metrics for the larger coffee supply chain. A.I. is why Emily knows when her online order will show up and can easily see the cost difference between the online store and the big box store.

As Miguel heads off to get coffee, A.I. fuels his navigation system, including the voice recognition system, the map app, and the navigation correction system he'll use to parallel park. But A.I. also impacts the roads he will drive on – from the predictive analysis system the transportation department uses to the population forecasting reports the city planners employ to determine the larger policy agenda.[10]

Smart machines impact who we date and how we fall in love. They shape where we live and how we find community. They impact our financial behavior in both small and large ways – from the tiny purchase we make online (like Miguel and Emily's pajama subscription) to the funds we choose for retirement. Smart algorithms impact our worldview and beliefs because of the new ways we receive our news. A.I. impacts the school board meetings and the polarization on social media through filter bubbles and echo chambers. In other words, A.I. is transforming the way that we think and behave and live.

The A.I. Revolution is already here. It's just that it's so normal, we don't really think of it as revolutionary. In other words, A.I. has become boring.

In this chapter, we'll explore three big realities about A.I. and how it impacts the classroom. Let's start with the notion that it's not actually an A.I. revolution.

THE A.I.
XEVOLUTION

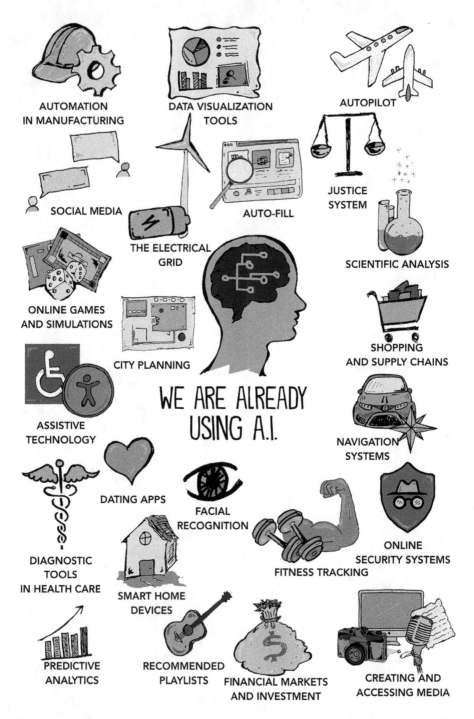

AUTOMATION
IN MANUFACTURING

DATA VISUALIZATION
TOOLS

AUTOPILOT

SOCIAL MEDIA

AUTO-FILL

JUSTICE
SYSTEM

THE ELECTRICAL
GRID

SCIENTIFIC ANALYSIS

ONLINE GAMES
AND SIMULATIONS

CITY PLANNING

SHOPPING
AND SUPPLY CHAINS

ASSISTIVE
TECHNOLOGY

WE ARE ALREADY
USING A.I.

NAVIGATION
SYSTEMS

DATING APPS

FACIAL
RECOGNITION

ONLINE
SECURITY SYSTEMS

DIAGNOSTIC
TOOLS
IN HEALTH CARE

FITNESS TRACKING

SMART HOME
DEVICES

PREDICTIVE
ANALYTICS

RECOMMENDED
PLAYLISTS

FINANCIAL MARKETS
AND INVESTMENT

CREATING AND
ACCESSING MEDIA

REALITY #1:
YOU ARE ALREADY USING A.I. IN YOUR CLASSROOM

While we tend to think of A.I. as a revolution, it's more like an evolution that's been at least seventy years in the making. The term "artificial intelligence" was first coined by John McCarthy, an American computer scientist, way back in 1956.[11] This was the era of punch cards and vacuum tubes. A computer often took up an entire room and users had to wear dust covers upon entering. Still, McCarthy envisioned a time when computer networks could engage in human-like cognition, ranging from recognizing images to understanding language to making decisions, to solving problems, to deeper creative thinking. What was once a dream of the 1950s slowly became a reality over the ensuing decades. Artificial intelligence works through algorithms, which are like sets of instructions that tell the computer what to do.

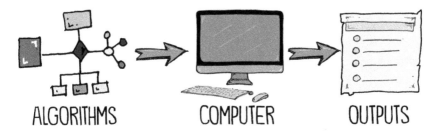

ALGORITHMS   COMPUTER   OUTPUTS

As mentioned before, these smart algorithms are all around us. Thus, if you're wondering, "How will A.I. change my classroom?" the short answer is, "It already has." A.I. fuels the spell checkers, grammar checkers, and the auto-fill functions your students use as they write. When they research using a search engine, that's also A.I. When you look at the weather to try and determine when to take your students out on a scavenger hunt, the meteorologists are using algorithms to predict weather patterns.

When your students take a standardized test, A.I. has already been a part of developing, testing, and re-norming the questions. If your school uses predictive analytics to find struggling students, that's also A.I. If your school uses a math or reading intervention program, there's a good chance it's an adaptive learning program centered on machine learning.

Before thinking about how A.I. is going to change your classroom, it might help to ask:

1. How has A.I. *already* changed the way we learn?
2. What are the pros and cons of using algorithms in learning?
3. What are the elements that have always remained the same even with the rise of A.I.?

When we recognize that A.I. is more of an evolution than a revolution, we are less likely to panic about the current changes taking place with generative A.I. We can recognize that A.I. is a powerful tool, and we don't want to take it lightly, but we also recognize that significant changes are often iterative. And yet, sometimes a new iteration is a huge leap, and we are in one of those phases where the newest trends in A.I. will have a huge impact on our lives.

REALITY #2:
GENERATIVE A.I. IS DIFFERENT

You've probably noticed that spell checker is significantly different from ChatGPT. That's because this newer generation of A.I. uses machine learning. This means the A.I. can learn from itself by refining how it makes predictions and performs tasks. Machine learning can be used for a wide range of tasks, such as image recognition, natural language processing, and fraud detection. There's an adaptive element to it.

But how do machines actually "learn?" Typically, they use one of the following three processes. Sometimes, it's a combination as well.

1. **Reinforcement learning:** A type of machine learning where the A.I. learns to make decisions in an environment by taking actions and receiving feedback in the form of rewards. So, an A.I. might learn how to play and win at chess or Go. Or a robot might learn how to navigate a maze.

2. **Supervised learning:** A type of machine learning where a model is trained using labeled data, meaning data where the correct output is already known, with the goal of making accurate predictions on new, unseen data. If you think about your spam filter in your email, this is supervised learning. The A.I. is trained on a data set of "spam" and "no spam" and learns how to analyze new examples to filter for spam.

3. **Unsupervised learning:** A type of machine learning where a model is trained on unlabeled data, meaning data where the correct output is not provided, with the goal of finding patterns or structure in the data. An example of this is fraud detection, where the A.I. discovers patterns and relationships in your purchase history with the hopes to flag anomalies.

I mentioned spell checker as an older type of A.I., but newer spell checks and grammar checks improve over time. If you've ever used auto-fill with sentence suggestions, you can see the difference between the older and newer forms of A.I.

About a decade ago, researchers began making enormous leaps in the development of a type of machine learning called deep learning. Deep learning uses artificial neural networks to process data. These networks are composed of layers of interconnected nodes that work together to learn from the data.

Deep learning can handle more complex tasks than traditional machine learning because it can process large amounts of data with many variables and features. Deep learning "trains" the algorithm to perform tasks by looking at multiple examples rather than programming an actual ask.

If you've used ChatGPT and thought, "This feels almost human-like," it's not an accident. These newer chatbots are designed that way. Deep learning relies on neural networks that mirror human cognition.

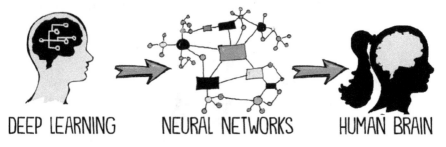

DEEP LEARNING   NEURAL NETWORKS   HUMAN BRAIN

We are training the machines **how to learn** rather than **how to do**. More recently, we have seen the emergence of generative A.I., which is a type of artificial intelligence that involves using machine learning algorithms to generate new data that resembles existing data. Hence the word *generative*.

This can include generating new text, images, music, or even videos in a similar style to existing content. If you've used an art generator, you'll see how you can create a prompt and it makes an entirely new picture in a style of your choosing. If you've used a chatbot, you've seen the potential for creating new text that mimics an existing author's style.

Not all generative A.I. techniques use deep learning. Some generative models use probabilistic models or other statistical techniques to generate new data. Others use a blend of probabilistic models with neural networks. But the key idea is that machines aren't merely thinking, they're thinking creatively.

If you have a hard time wrapping your brain around this, don't worry. I've talked to dozens of computer scientists and A.I. architects, and I still don't completely understand how A.I. works. But what we do need to recognize is that these smart machines feel more human than ever.

And they're not going away.

REALITY #3
A.I. IS HERE TO STAY

Generative A.I. is still in its infancy. Most of the tools and platforms mentioned in this book will be either updated or obsolete within the next year. I deliberately avoided writing a book about ChatGPT because I knew ChatGPT-4 would arrive sometime during my writing process. Sure enough, I'm using ChatGPT-4 on a daily basis.

A.I. will continue to transform our practice in ways that surprise us. Therefore, we will need to be adaptable as we face new challenges and possibilities. We will need to experiment and iterate. Fortunately, this is what we, as educators, do every day. We adapt to new challenges (just think of the pandemic). We modify our lessons to meet the needs of our students. We try new strategies and test new ideas. If you're a teacher, you're already an innovator.

As we move forward in this uncertain terrain, we need to think wisely about the role of A.I. in our lives in both negative and positive ways. We know that machine learning will have a major impact on our students and in the way they learn.

It can help to ask the question, "What is it that A.I. does well?" and "What does A.I. do poorly?" The following two sketchnotes are a brief explanation of what A.I. does well and what it does poorly. As you view them, please consider what this might mean for your students and for your role as a teacher.

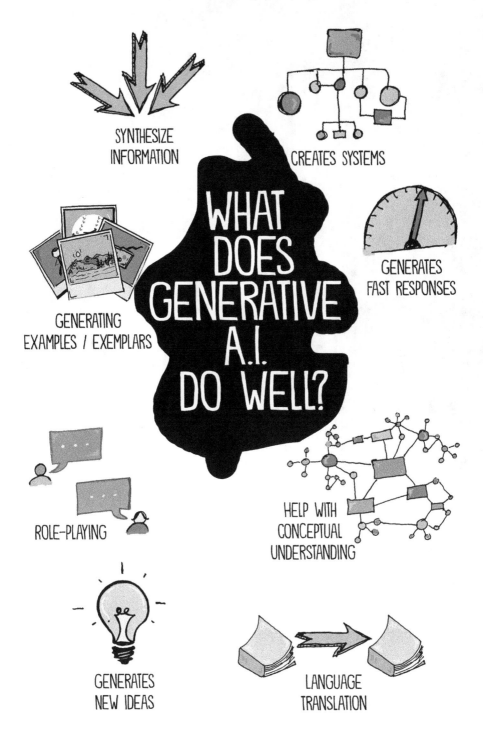

EMPATHY
AND EMOTIONAL
INTELLIGENCE

ADAPTIVE
THINKING

CONTEXTUAL
UNDERSTANDING

REAL-TIME KNOWLEDGE

WHAT DOES GENERATIVE A.I. DO POORLY?

FACTUAL
ACCURACY

DIVERGENT
THINKING

ETHICAL
THINKING

VOICE

KNOWING THE LIMITATIONS OF ARTIFICIAL INTELLIGENCE

While A.I. is certainly not limited to chatbots, I'd like to explore its limitations for a moment. If you log into ChatGPT, the home screen makes it clear what the chatbot does well and what it does poorly. I've taken their initial list and expanded it with some additional limitations.

- **ChatGPT is often dated**. Its neural network relies on information that stops at 2021. This means ChatGPT lacks understanding of emerging knowledge.
- **ChatGPT can be inaccurate.** It will make things up to fill in the gaps. This could be due to misinformation in the vast data set it pulls from. But it might also be an unintended consequence of the inherent creativity in A.I. When a tool has the potential to generate new content, there is always the potential that the new content might contain misinformation.[12]
- **ChatGPT may contained biased content**. Like all machine learning models, ChatGPT may reflect the biases in its training data. This means that it may give responses that reflect societal biases, such as gender or racial biases, even if unintentionally.[13] [14] Many of the A.I. systems used the Enron data files as an initial language training. The emails, which were in public domain, contained a more authentic form of speech. But it was also a form of speech that skewed conservative and male because Enron was a Texas-based energy company.[15]
- **ChatGPT lacks contextual knowledge.** While ChatGPT can analyze the words in each sentence or paragraph, it may not always understand the context in which those words are used. This can lead to responses that are technically correct but don't make sense in the larger conversation. If a student writes a personal narrative, they know the context better than any

A.I. could possibly understand. When writing about local issues for a school newspaper or blog, the A.I. won't have the local knowledge that a student journalism team demonstrates. Therefore, it's critical that students learn how to contextualize knowledge.

- **ChatGPT requires an understanding of command prompts.** This sounds simple but it's easy to miss. ChatGPT isn't a mind reader, so if students use it to answer questions, they need to be adept at designing their command prompts.
- **ChatGPT lacks empathy.** ChatGPT may not be able to understand the emotional context of conversations. This can lead to inappropriate or insensitive responses.
- **ChatGPT lacks common sense.** I'm not sure how to describe this but some of the answers I've gotten on ChatGPT seem silly and nonsensical. ChatGPT's responses are based solely on the patterns and associations it has learned from text data. It may not always have the common sense or practical knowledge to provide accurate responses.
- **ChatGPT might not be eco-friendly.** Deep learning requires an immense amount of processing power. As A.I. becomes more pervasive, there's the potential it could accelerate climate change. *Wired Magazine* described it this way, "deep learning inherently requires huge swathes of data, and though innovations in chips mean we can do that faster and more efficiently than ever, there's no question that A.I. research churns through energy."[16] On the other hand, certain technologists have looked toward A.I. as a potential solution for making power grids more efficient and reducing the amount of energy we collectively consume.

WHAT DOES THIS MEAN
FOR OUR STUDENTS?

If A.I. can think like a human in a way that is faster and more comprehensive, what does that mean for our students? Are we merely preparing them to become a slower, more human, version of A.I.? Should we focus solely on the human skills that A.I. doesn't do well (like empathy and contextual understanding)? Or is there still a place for things like writing or coding?

In the next chapter, we ask the question, "If A.I. can do it, should students even bother?" We'll focus on two potential dead ends that we want to avoid as we design our A.I. roadmap. Finally, we'll explore a third way that embraces both the human element and machine learning.

CHAPTER 3

HOW WILL SCHOOLS RESPOND TO A.I.?

Yesterday, I asked Chat GPT-4 to write an essay response to a high-interest writing prompt of "Will we ever have flying cars in the future?"

> Flying cars have been a popular idea and a staple of science fiction for many years. While it's difficult to predict the future with certainty, it is unlikely that we will have flying cars in the near future.
>
> There are several reasons for this. First and foremost, the technology required to create safe and reliable flying cars simply does not exist yet. While there have been advances in aviation technology, creating a flying car that is both efficient and safe for everyday use is a significant challenge that has not yet been overcome.
>
> Secondly, even if we were able to develop the necessary technology, there are many regulatory and logistical hurdles that would need to be addressed before flying cars could become a reality. For example, air traffic control systems would need to be overhauled to accommodate thousands of flying cars sharing the skies with commercial planes and helicopters. Additionally, new regulations and licensing requirements would need to be put in place to ensure that drivers of flying cars are properly trained and licensed to operate them safely.
>
> Finally, there are also environmental and social considerations to take into account. Flying cars would likely require significant amounts of energy to operate and could have a negative impact on air quality and noise pollution in urban areas. In summary, while the idea of flying cars is certainly exciting, it is unlikely that we will see them become a reality in the near future due to significant technological, regulatory, and environmental challenges.

I then modified it to be the style of a middle schooler. Here was the result:

> Flying cars have been a hot topic for a long time, but it's not very likely that we're going to see them on the streets anytime soon. The main problem is that creating a car that can fly and be safe at the same time is really tough, and we just don't have the technology for it yet. Yeah, we've made some progress in aviation, but getting a flying car that can be efficient and safe for everyday use is a big challenge that we haven't been able to conquer.
>
> And even if we were able to create the technology, there would be a whole bunch of new rules and regulations we'd need to put in place to make sure that people knew how to use them and that they

weren't causing any problems for other airplanes or creating too much pollution. The air traffic control system would need to be revamped to handle all the new traffic from flying cars, and we'd need to make sure that the people driving them are properly trained and licensed.

Plus, let's not forget about the environmental and social impact of flying cars. They would use a ton of energy and could create a lot of noise and pollution in urban areas. We'd need to figure out how to make them eco-friendly and socially acceptable before they could be a regular part of our daily lives. So, while it would be super cool to have flying cars like in the movies, it's probably not going to happen anytime soon. We've got a lot of challenges to overcome first.

This took all of three minutes to accomplish. It's only going to get faster and more individualized in the upcoming years. Critics are already point out that this is the end of the essay as we know it. Similarly, in the STEM / STEAM world, I've already seen pundits claim that we no longer need to teach programming if A.I. can do a better job than our students. [17] [18]

What does this mean for us as educators? How will we respond to this new reality? There are two main dead ends that we need to consider.

DEAD END #1
THE HYPED-UP PROMISE OF TECHNO FUTURISM

The first dead end is Techno Futurism. This is a full embrace of A.I. to transform education. It's the idea that we should redesign education from the ground up using technology as the catalyst for change. Techno Futurism isn't a new philosophy. We've heard the same thing with one-to-one devices, adaptive learning programs, and flipped videos.[19] The Techno Futurist jumps from one promising technology to the next with bold claims about how it will change learning forever.

Currently, the emerging technology is A.I. Who needs direct instruction if students can ask a chatbot an endless array of questions and receive personalized answers? Who needs assessment if an A.I. can give targeted feedback? Who needs to write an essay of machine learning can do it faster and perhaps even better?

We've seen bold predictions about A.I. destroying the essay and causing the end of English Language Arts. The Techno Fururist embraces these ideas in the name of "disruption." Some Techno Futurists will even go so far as to claim that A.I. will eventually replace teachers.

For the Techno Futurist, generative A.I. is a chance to reimagine education in a world of smart machines. It's an opportunity to leverage these powerful technology tools to do the low-level thinking so that our students can engage in nonstop critical thinking.

Techno futurism looks at the transformative power of A.I. and asks, "What learning tasks can Artificial Intelligence replace?"

But I think this misses the point

Just because you *can* automate something doesn't mean you *should* automate it.

JUST BECAUSE
YOU CAN
AUTOMATE THE TASK
DOESN'T MEAN
YOU SHOULD
AUTOMATE THE TASK

ALMOST ANY TASK CAN BE AUTOMATED BUT WHERE'S THE JOY IN THAT?

Some tasks are simply fun to do, even if they can be automated and mechanized in a way that's faster and cheaper. You can buy a blanket at a big box store. It's fast and cheap. Or you can crochet it and spend more time and money along the way. But it's that crocheted blanket from a close friend that you will cherish forever.

You can buy a pitching machine and never need to play catch with your kid again. However, you'll be missing out on one of the best parts of parenthood. You can use navigation to get around a city, but you can also put your phone away and discover a new city by chasing your curiosity by foot. Sure, a map app can do a better job getting you there efficiently but is efficiency always the bottom line?

My son Micah is really into art. He can hop onto an A.I. digital art generator and get a finished work in a matter of seconds. But guess what? He still loves making art from scratch. Similarly, a student can easily 3D print an object after using a digital modeling program, but that same student might just come alive when given a block clay and the challenge of forming something entirely by hand.

I love to write. Even if the A.I. does a better and faster job than me, I'm a writer. I need write. It feeds my soul. If I go too many days in a row without writing, I feel lost. Writing makes me feel alive.

When the pandemic hit, I asked my students to do a show and tell activity with the prompt, "What is one healthy way you are coping with social isolation?"

One by one, they held their items up to the camera and described their healthy coping mechanism. They talked of gardening, baking cookies, painting pictures, journaling, writing songs, computer coding, and doing word puzzles. Nearly every activity they chose was something that could be automated. These tasks that could so easily have been outsourced were a lifeline when students faced social isolation.

About a decade ago, Dean Shareski argued that joy is not merely a means to learning. Joy is an end in itself. In his TED Talk, he argued that we need more joy in schools.[20]

Shareski argued that joy is a necessary human need and schools should cultivate that in students. But what about the educational value of these tasks? What happens to learning when we rely too heavily on a machine?

IF WE OUTSOURCE EVERY TASK, WE MIGHT SHORT-CIRCUIT THE LEARNING

Often, the very task that can be outsourced to an A.I. is a strategy we still need use to engage in deeper learning. For a few years now, photo based A.I. apps have been able to solve complex algorithms in math class. But the act of looking at a problem, formulating the equation, and solving it is a critical part of mathematical thinking. If we never work through the process, we fail to develop the systemic thinking and number sense we need as mathematical thinkers.

It's true that A.I. can already replace the traditional high school English essay. But the goal of an essay isn't merely to write a great essay. The act of writing is a critical part of how we make meaning. There's a false assumption that we learn content and then demonstrate our learning through writing. But the act of writing is often a key component to how we think and how we learn. We learn *through* our writing process.

An A.I. can take a complex informational text and distill it down to a series of notes in history class. But a hand drawn sketch note helps create the synaptic connections needed to move the information from short term to long term memory. You become a better conceptual thinker when you don't use A.I. for notetaking. If we look at this diagram of information processing, we need students to get information into their long-term memory:

INFORMATION PROCESSING DIAGRAM

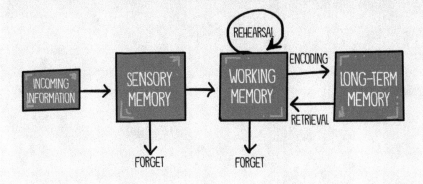

Adapted from Atkinson, R.C. and Shiffrin, R.M. (1968) 'Human memory: a proposed system and its control processes.' In Spence, KW. and Spence J.T. *The psychology of learning and motivation, (v. 2).* New York: Academic Press. pp. 89-195.

Research has demonstrated that students retain more information when they take notes by hand rather than typing them by hand.[21] Similarly, students become better observers in science when they sketch out what they see. The act of drawing teaches students how to observe. We need students to "make thinking visible" (a term developed by Ron Ritchart and Mark Church).[22] Students need to play with information in every stage of the thinking process.

A student can use a calculator, but they benefit from doing math by hand or engaging in mental math. Does it mean we ban calculators? Nope. It just means we use a mix of strategies. We might use manipulatives, sketches, calculators, and even slide rules. That last option might seem like a joke but it's not. A slide rule can help students see the progression of math. We need to avoid this Techno Futurist dead end. But sometimes in doing so, we turn the opposite direction and run into the second dead end of the Lock It and Block It approach.

DEAD END #2
THE LOCK IT AND BLOCK IT APPROACH

"Mr. Spencer, I can't talk to my group members," a student called out.

"What do you mean?" I asked.

"Look, the chat's gone," Carlos pointed to his computer.

"Gone, gone?" I asked.

"Mine, too," another student chimed in.

"Yeah, it's not showing up for me, either." I was met with a chorus of "mine won't work as well."

"No worries, just send an email to your Global Voice teammates."

This time, their emails were rejected. Nothing seemed to work.

"I got it to work on my phone," another student said. "I just had to use my personal Gmail, instead."

Suddenly, students started using alternate emails and tethering to one another's hot spots. Meanwhile, I couldn't figure out what was happening.

That afternoon, I met with tech support and learned that the district had disabled chat and limited emails back and forth due to bullying that had occurred in another classroom. My students were working on a global collaboration project and suddenly they couldn't collaborate with their teammates.

This was the Lock It and Block It approach, focused on surveillance, accountability measures, and blocking any technology that might be used inappropriately.

In terms of generative A.I., I'm already seeing certain teachers saying things like, "I'll just make students handwrite all their essays in class." But as Mary Beth Hertz brought up, this strategy can be ableist.[23] Some students simply need to type their work. In an upcoming chapter, we'll explore how students can use A.I. tools for scaffolds and supports. If we simply ban all A.I. from the classroom, we remove a tool that can increase accessibility to deeper learning.

While true it's true students can use A.I. for cheating, they can also use it as a powerful learning tool. In building background knowledge, students can ask specific questions and get personalized answers. They can ask follow-up questions and engage in a dialogue.

In math, a student might ask a chatbot what is and isn't a polynomial. From there, they can continue to ask clarifying questions as they develop deeper mathematical understanding. In writing, there might be times when students start out with A.I. and then modify and rework it to have their own unique voice and style.

A.I. has the power to help synthesize information, clarify misconceptions, and provide tutorials for skill practice. It can help us get unstuck during writer's block. A.I. can be an excellent tool in converting a complex text into one at a more accessible reading level or in translating it into another language. A.I. can help students who struggle with executive function break down tasks into smaller to-do lists.

When we focus solely on how A.I. might be misused as a tool for cheating, we fail to recognize its power in helping students learning — especially those who are the most vulnerable.

To be clear, we need to follow the laws and policies on educational technology. We need to take privacy laws seriously. I live in the USA, where we need to make sure all apps are COPA[24] and CIPA[25] compliant. But we can't move forward from a place of fear and reactivity.

In the upcoming years, our students will need to learn how to use these tools wisely. If we completely lock down all generative A.I., we run the risk of not helping students see what it means to wrestle the hard questions about how A.I. is shaping our world.

We miss out on the opportunity to teach a new kind of digital citizenship and help students develop a critical eye needed for information literacy in an age of smart machines. A Lock It and Block It approach won't help students learn to use these tools wisely and ethically.

A.I. IS A POWERFUL TOOL
BLOCKING IT WON'T HELP STUDENTS LEARN HOW TO USE IT WISELY

BUT THERE IS A THIRD WAY

THIS IS THE
HUMAN
APPROACH

Techno Futurism fixates on novelty rather than sustainability. It ignores the negative aspects of technology. Meanwhile, the Lock It and Block It approach leads to irrelevance. So, where does that leave us?

There's a third option.

The answer can be found in taking a vintage innovation approach.[26] With vintage innovation, we avoid the extremes of a reactionary "just block it all" approach as well as the naivety of futurism. Here, we mash up the old school and the new tech. We overlay best and next practices. We ask, "what does it mean to do human work in a tech-centric world?"

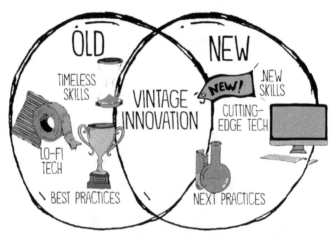

Vintage innovation is the process of taking established ideas and concepts and updating them in a new and innovative way. This can involve reusing, repurposing, or adapting older technologies or designs to create something new and improved. Vintage innovation often draws on the past for inspiration, while also incorporating modern design principles. In terms of A.I., a vintage innovation approach is human-driven but tech-informed.

USE IT WISELY

The best creators are going to know how to use A.I. in a way that still allows them to retain their humanity. This feels like a daunting task, but I'm inspired by a phenomenon in competitive chess. A.I. will nearly always beat a human. But when you do chess via teams, the fully automated A.I. teams rarely win. Neither do the all-human teams. The winning teams are nearly always the combination of A.I. and human.[27]

Consider a programmer. She might outsource the easier code to A.I. and focus on the most challenging code herself. She might doublecheck her work with A.I. She might ask the A.I. for help with certain questions or ideas. She might even start with the A.I. code and then edit it to make it more efficient or to take it in a new direction.

A digital artist might ask the A.I. to do five different pictures and then he uses that as an inspiration for his own work. He might take two different sample images and mash them up in a sort of collage art. He might turn the A.I. off completely and work on something from scratch and then later try digital modeling just to see the difference between the two approaches.

A mathematician might attempt a problem and then use A.I. to doublecheck their work. They might take handwritten notes and ask questions aloud as the teacher models how to find the p-value. But later, that same student might use a chatbot to clarify the information.

Sounds scary? Exciting? Chances are you're feeling both. I am, too. Like many people, I've been surprised by how powerful this tool can be. Which is why, in the end, the question, "Will A.I. replace this learning task?" might actually be the wrong question. A better question might be, "How will A.I. *change* this learning task?"

IN A WORLD OF A.I.,
OUR STUDENTS WILL NEED TO
BECOME REALLY GOOD
AT WHAT AI CAN'T DO AND
REALLY DIFFERENT
WITH WHAT IT CAN DO.

FOCUS ON THE HUMAN SKILLS

In *Human Work in an Age of Smart Machines*, Jamie Merisotis argues that we should begin with the question, "What is it that we, as humans, can do that machines can't do?"[28] It might mean developing empathy, thinking divergently, engaging in curiosity, finding your own unique lens, or coming up with innovative solutions.

Here's the good news. Countless schools around the world have already developed Graduate Profiles. These profiles outline the knowledge, skills, and competencies that students should possess upon completing their K-12 education.

In other words, these graduate profiles are looking at the human skills that students will need in an age of machine learning. But a graduate profile cannot simply remain a document that schools house on a website or a poster they hang on classroom walls. If students are going to develop these deeply human skills, we will need to rethink the type of learning that students engage in. We'll need to de-emphasize (and perhaps even scrap) standardized testing and emphasize human skills. We will need to focus on changing our instructional practices so that students develop those key competencies within the graduate profiles.

In our book *Empower*, AJ Juliani and I shared how the corporate ladder is now a maze. For years, we learned the formula that we should work hard in school, graduate from a university, and climb a corporate ladder.[29] This was never the reality for everyone. Some folks found success in trade schools. Others as entrepreneurs. Meanwhile, systemic racism, gender bias, and injustice created barriers for millions of marginalized people.

However, it was the formula we were taught. But with the changes in automation and machine learning, the ladder is now a maze. Our students will need to develop deeply human skills in an age of smart machines. They will need to develop empathy, resilience, divergent thinking, communication skills, curation skills, a better mindset around media literacy, and creativity.

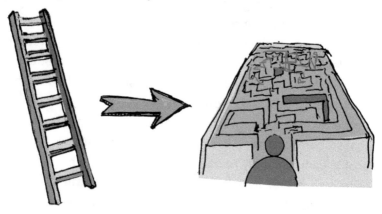

Pundits have long said, "We need to prepare students for the jobs that don't exist yet." But we've already seen how quickly this falls into trap of Techno Futurism. A decade ago, it was all about teaching every student how to code. Now a chatbot can produce seemingly flawless code in seconds.

Our students will navigate this maze of an uncertain future. Part of this navigation will involve thinking critically about the pros and cons of when to use A.I. (as previously mentioned). Some of it will involve thinking critically about A.I. and how it is changing our world (an idea we explore in Chapter 5). Much of this navigation will involve developing critical human skills that machines cannot do. But it will also involve empowering our students with a sense of ownership over their journey. Here, they will embrace the idea of being different.

BE DIFFERENT

Artificial Intelligence can do many things well, but it can't capture your unique voice. Earlier I mentioned that students will need to become really good at the things A.I. can't do (those deeply human skills we just explored) and different at what A.I. can do. But what do we mean by different?

Think of it this way. A drum machine is great, but the slight imperfections and quirky idiosyncrasies are why I love listening to Keith Moon riff on old records from The Who.

When we write, our humor and humanity, in all its imperfections, make it worth sharing. I can take some of Grammarly's A.I.-generated suggestions to clean up my writing, but I need to do so carefully. I'm messy and loquacious. I'm overly conversational in my tone. But that's me. And if I'm going to write a book, it needs to be my voice – flaws and all.

I love to draw. Artificial Intelligence can create far better drawings than what I share. But when you watch my sketch videos or see a slide on a keynote I deliver or look at an image on my Instagram, you see me. In other words, A.I. can make great digital art but it can't make *my* art.

Culturally, we tend to think of math as being cold and logical, talk to a mathematician and they'll tell you about the beauty and poetry in solving a math problem. There's a personal style that mathematicians bring to their craft that a computer cannot replicate.

In an era of A.I., voice and choice are more important than ever. We don't know what types of jobs our students will eventually do. But we do know that they will need to think differently if they want to stand apart. As we continue through this book, we will be highlighting what it means to take a human-centered approach in a world of A.I. But first, I'd like to share a completely fictional A.I. story.

CHAPTER 4
MENDING THE TEARS IN A SUPER SUIT
(A SHORT STORY)

Six months ago, Rose thought it was a prank. Some kind of avant-garde exhibit from the Humanities department. Put the engineering kids through a weird experience and call it art. But after reviewing the technology and the classified documents, she now accepted all of it as real – the heroes, the superpowers, the comic books she poured over as a kid (and still poured over as a college sophomore). It was real. All of it.

Someday, she might become a lead engineer designing the next generation of devices for heroes. She'd be in a graphic novel. Okay, maybe not her. But her inventions would be there. They'd probably make her a generic figure in a lab coat. Maybe she'd be an eccentric old man with gray hair. But who cares? The invention would remain for the entire series immortalized in print.

So far, she was number one on the leaderboard. She had fixed major flaws in seemingly broken technology. She had solved huge design challenges in the VR simulation room.

But now that she'd leveled up, she would be providing simple technology help for current heroes. How hard could that be? If she aced ten house calls, she could move on as a full-time R&D intern and from there? Who knows? Someday she might run this lab.

But not today. Today, she would provide basic instructions to a hero who couldn't manage to get his Geer App to work on his tablet.

Rose walked across the winding driveway and trudged up the steps. "Remember, these are action heroes, not thinking heroes," she whispered to herself.

She took a deep breath and pressed the doorbell.

"Hello there," a gentle voice answered. It was nothing like the booming voice she had seen in the movies.

"I'm from Geer Industries."

"Swell! Come right in." The door handle jiggled. "Oh, that's right. It's automatic. There's a button for this somewhere."

The screen above the doorbell flashed on. Rose studied the man in the pastel yellow cardigan as he pulled out a pair of glasses and leaned in toward the camera. He looked to be in his mid-twenties, but he dressed like her great grandfather.

"Please excuse the delay. I'm afraid the buttons aren't labeled," he said leaning into the camera. He moved so methodically for a hero with super speed.

"Don't worry. Just push any of the buttons," Rose said.

"What if it's a wrong button?" his voice faltered.

"You'll be fine," she answered.

He ran his hands through perfectly combed hair. "I can do this," he mumbled as he waved his finger around the touchscreen. Finally, he shrugged and tapped a button. The porch light turned on.

"Well, that's not it," he muttered. "That'll do me no good in the midday sun, now will it?"

"I can help you with this," Rose said in the perkiest voice she could muster. Her phone buzzed. She tapped on the screen and an image popped up of the Geer Industries Hero Home Security System interface.

The man in the cardigan clicked another button and the sprinklers turned on.

"Okay, it's the third button down on the left," she said as she looked up from her screen and sidestepped the staccato stream from the sprinkler.

"Got it," he said, clicking the button.

Right then, five lasers pointed at Rose's forehead. A high-pitched alarm began chirping.

"Initiating intruder destruction mode," a robotic voice warned. Both the voice and the alarm were far too friendly for the present reality.

Rose's heart raced. The facial recognition program was supposed to override this type of human error. How could it fail? She'd tested it nineteen times in the lab. The A.I. even told her she had a "strong jaw line," which was supposed to be a compliment, right?

It shouldn't be doing this.

"Did you press the third button down on the left?" Rose asked.

"Oh, my left? I assumed it was your left," he answered.

"Why would you think that?" Rose asked.

"Nine seconds," the robotic voice said.

"There's a red override button. It's bright red. Can't miss it," she said.

"Eight seconds," the robotic voice calmly spoke.

"I don't see any buttons. It's all just a flat screen," he answered.

"Yes, the flat screen. There's a button."

"You mean the red square?"

"Yes, the red square. That's the override. Press it," she yelled.

"Three . . . two . . ."

Rose braced for the impact. Her first service call and she'd be incinerated. Click! The door flew open. The chirping ceased.

"That was close," the man said.

Rose fell forward, still holding her breath. She still couldn't speak.

"I'm Frank. And by that I mean my name and not my character. I tend to be more subtle than frank," he said, holding out a sweaty hand. She shook it and offered a nervous smile.

"I'm Rose. And by that I mean my name and not my hue," she answered.

"Aside from your hair," he said with a smile.

She brushed her pink bangs away from her face.

He continued, "When I was your age, I begged my mother to allow me to color my hair pink but she refused. Times were different."

"I'm here to help you install the Geer Industries app on your devices and to make sure . . ."

"Oh, drat. I think I provided you with my alter-ego name rather than my hero name," Frank interrupted.

"I already knew your alter-ego name," Rose said as they walked across the massive entryway, through a corridor, and toward the kitchen. "I know all about you. I've read about every villain you defeated. I read and re-read every one of your graphic novels when I was little. You seemed to just disappear. You almost hit public domain but then we learned you were frozen and then that movie came out and . . ."

"Did you say graphic novel? I'm not a novelist and if I were, I doubt I would write anything violent enough to be graphic," Frank said. "I would go character-driven and bucolic."

"Sorry, comics. I read your comic books," Rose said. She knew his entire backstory. His super speed. His ability to breath under water. The way they cryogenically froze him after World War II to preserve him in an emergency in case of a nuclear disaster during the Cold War.

"Would you like a beverage?"

"I'm good," Rose answered.

"I have some hot chocolate," he added. "You know, they have this swell new machine that makes the hot chocolate all by itself. You just grab a tiny plastic cup and voila! The wonders! But I prefer my homemade recipe. Are you sure you wouldn't like to try it? It's the cat's pajamas if you ask me."

"Well, maybe I could . . ."

He snapped his finger. "I'll take that as a less than enthusiastic yes. Now, let me see here. This is what they call a smart kitchen. I have an assistant. She's an invisible electrical ghost servant who helps me open drawers and whatnot. I'm perfectly capable of trifling through the kitchen myself but Geer Industries insists I make use of the virtual assistant. I believe her name is Val."

"How can I help you?" an automated voice spoke.

"I don't mean to bother you. I feel terribly sorry that I spoke your name right then."

"I am at your service," she answered.

"I find that unnerving, don't you?" he whispered. "I've never been comfortable with the idea of servants."

"She's just an A.I. program," Rose said. "It's all a part of machine learning. You should see some of the programs they're developing in the lab."

Frank opened a cupboard and reached for a mug. "Machine learning? Well, that's a term I've never heard. At the rate of technological development, we may no longer need superpowers in the future. I've never really considered that."

Her phone vibrated. A message popped up.

They're action heroes, not thinking heroes. Change the subject.

"It's not a big deal," Rose answered.

"Well, I think that's a significant development, don't you? At what point is a superpower even necessary?" he asked.

She glanced at her phone. A new message popped up. *Get him to change the subject. Now.*

"The hot chocolate smells amazing," she said.

"Thank you, I've always loved baking but never had the time for it," he said, as searched through a drawer. "It's a new home and I haven't the slightest idea where anything is. But I did manage to whip this hot cocoa up a few hours ago. The key is to let it steep but not burn. The magical ingredient isn't love. It's time."

He continued to rummage through the drawers in frustration mumbling the word "ladle."

"You might want to ask your trusted virtual assistant," Rose said. "I can help you with any reconfigurations if you'd like."

He waved her off.

"You know, when I was young, we had a group of heroes that warned about the technology thing. They were a bit reactive, to be fair. They wouldn't even use a basic grappling hook. Felt like you should do everything with your bare hands and whatnot. They claimed that someday the technology would replace all the heroes. We wrote them off as crazy but I'm starting to think they had a point."

"You know, Val might be able to help you with find what you're looking for," Rose said.

"Did you hear that?" he asked.

"What?" Rose asked.

"The electric ghost lady didn't speak to you when you said her name," he pointed out.

"That's by default. She's programmed to recognize your voice."

"But what if I change it to a Mid-Atlantic accent?" he asked in an old-timey radio voice.

"You'll have to try that out," Rose said.

He looked up in the air and spoke in a thick southern accent, "Dearest Val, I hate to be an inconvenience, but would you happen to know where the ladle is?"

A drawer opened slowly. A ladle began to float above the counter. Frank's eyes widened.

"She really is a ghost," he said.

"It's just magnets," Rose said. "Nothing special. Our lab has a whole line of magnetic gadgets."

"You know, magnetics was a significant superpower when I was a child. This is what I mean. The technology might replace us." His face grew somber. "We had a hero named Magnetron. That was her power. I don't know what she would do if she were still alive. Go out and become an accountant?"

Rose's phone buzzed again. *Distract him. Get him off this line of reasoning.*

"We'll always need heroes with powers," Rose said as Frank ladled the hot chocolate into an enormous mug. "There are several heroes right now who combine their magnetic powers creatively with the Geer Industries technology. It didn't replace their powers. It just enhanced it."

"I suppose," Frank said as waved her over to the next room. "Here's the family room. I've never had a family of my own. Maybe I should call it the living room. Then again, living room wouldn't fit well for a man who hasn't had much of a life," he said with an awkward laugh.

"You single-handedly took down . . ."

He waved his hand dismissively. "You're talking about Swift Strike. But in this moment, I'm Frank and Frank was frozen for years while his friends and family continued living. That was the first thing I did when they woke me up. I called every number. I remembered them by heart. One by one, I went through my mental list until I real-ized I was all alone. Most of them had died."

Rose's phone vibrated. She tapped on the screen and read the alert. *You need to get him to stop talking.*

"Let's figure out how to configure your Geer Industries app. Should we start with your tablet?" Rose asked.

"Tablet?" he raised an eyebrow, then shrugged his shoulders and grabbed a yellow legal pad.

"No, a different kind of tablet. I'm referring to the flat screen that works like a computer," Rose said.

"That's right. Yes, the tablet. It's on the table," Frank said as he placed the mugs on a silver tray. He maneuvered around the mahog-any furniture and opened the curtains to reveal a floor to ceiling window with a breathtaking view of the city. He stared out for what felt like an eternity.

Rose sat still on the couch. Her phone vibrated again but she didn't pick it up.

Turning to Rose, Frank waved his hand at the city skyline and said, "There's so much of this city I've never explored."

"Why don't you?" Rose asked.

"It's hard to make plans when you're always on call. Even harder to make friends," he lamented.

Another message popped up. *Get him to grab the tablet.*

"So, I'd love to check out your tablet and show you how we can integrate the tablet, your phone, your super suit and your home into one single ecosystem," Rose said.

He winced in embarrassment. "I'm sorry for keeping you waiting. You must have places you need to go and more important service calls."

Rose turned toward the coffee table and grabbed the mug from the silver tray. She pulled it up to her trembling hands. All at once, the mug slipped and careened toward the floor. Rose jumped back to see Frank holding the mug on a saucer with one hand. She blinked twice and stared at him.

She had read about it in the comic books. She had seen his superpower in full CGI splendor at the movie theater. But this happened without the blurry light or the whooshing sound of the movies. This was his super speed. The silence made it feel even more impressive.

"Did you just use your superpower?" she whispered.

"You didn't see anything," he said with a sly smile.

Rose could barely manage to shake her head.

"Well, I couldn't let you spill my homemade hot chocolate, now, could I? Not on such a beautiful cashmere sweater," he added as he grabbed the tablet from the table.

"Thank you," she said. The truth is, she hated the sweater. She normally wore a hoodie and jeans but she wasn't sure what to wear when doing tech help for a hero.

Her phone buzzed again. *Nicely done. Keep it focused on the tech.*

Rose cleared her throat. "Let's see. It looks like you have an Android."

"I have no such thing," he said. "I know an android when I see one. I once took down an entire squadron of Nazi androids during the war."

"I'm sorry. I was referring to your tablet."

"It's a Nazi tablet?" he asked.

"No, it's the name of it. Just, um, could you enter your passcode for me?" she asked.

He entered his passcode (1234) and pointed to the screen. "You know, I need to get these pictures into my computer. Could you help me with that?" he asked, pointing to the photo album.

Rose knew this was beyond the scope of her tech help but what could it hurt?

"See this icon?" she asked.

He nodded.

"Hold your finger on it and wait for the menu to show up. Then move down to 'transfer to laptop.' And that's it."

"That's it?" he asked.

"That's it," she said with a smile.

"Are they really on my computer?" he asked.

"Well, they are in the cloud."

He cocked his head to the side. "I don't see how water vapor could store data."

"It's not really a cloud. It's a network of . . . it's hard to explain." How could she explain the internet to someone who had been frozen in time since 1949?

"You know, I've always wanted to be an artist," he said. He opened the album and flipped through the screen.

Rose's phone vibrated. *Get him back on track. Focus on the Geer app.*

"Well, your pictures are beautiful, but the world needs heroes."

"You really think they're beautiful?" he asked.

"Of course," Rose lied. The pictures were actually derivative and boring, but you can't just say that to a stranger; especially one who has discovered art as the only temporary salve to the crushing pain of human loneliness.

Rose continued, "The important thing to remember is that the world needs heroes."

"I'm not so sure," he said. "Have you heard of climate change?"

Rose nodded.

"I can't take down climate change," he pointed out.

"Well, yeah, sure, but you have super speed. You have a gift. The world needs that gift," Rose said, trying to channel the advice of every single comic book monolog she had read so many times the binding fell apart.

"But isn't art a gift?" he asked.

"Yes, but you have literally saved the world," Rose said.

The app. Get him to download the app.

"And you don't think art can save the world?" he asked.

"You have a superpower that no one else has. You can do what no one else can do."

"Is that really true, though? When I was a child, we had Danger Drone. He had this gorgeous black and yellow suit. I was so jealous. It was so slick. But now they have unmanned drones flown by someone sitting in an airconditioned room sipping on an energy drink and none of it matters because our insatiable thirst for consumption means polar bears are stuck on tiny blocks of ice and somehow the entire western U.S. is now on fire. And I heard that someday the A.I. will be able to fly the drones themselves. We won't even need anyone sitting in an office drinking an energy drink."

"I see," was all Rose could muster.

He buried his head in his hands.

"Are you okay?" Rose asked.

Frank was sobbing in heavy convulsions. Rose wasn't sure what to do. Give him an awkward side hug? Call for help? Grab a box of tissues? Instead, she simply sat on the sofa, two feet away from him while he cried.

Rose's phone vibrated repeatedly. Messages popped up so quickly she couldn't read a single one.

Finally, he stopped and wiped his tears and snot with a silk handkerchief he had kept in his pocket. "I'm terribly sorry. I'm just not sure I can keep doing this."

"Let's just focus on learning how to use the app," Rose said. For the next two hours, she walked him through the Geer Industries app. She taught him how to track his stats, how to order repairs on his suit, and how to communicate with fellow heroes in the private network. She walked him through the configurations of Val and taught him how to make a nostalgic playlist of the songs of his college days. By the end, he seemed outright excited about the new technology.

Rose drove back to the lab with the nagging question of whether A.I. would essentially erase all human error in people. And if so, would that be such a bad thing? Did we really want to place the fate of humanity in the hands of a hero who can't figure out how to get pictures off a tablet and onto a laptop or who suddenly starts bawling his eyes out? Then again, do we want to leave decision-making in the hands of smart machines incapable of bawling their eyes out and experiencing an existential crisis?

Rose snaked her way through the city streets until she reached the underground parking garage where she rolled down the window for the facial recognition scan.

The light remained red.

"What is this?" she asked. Was the A.I. somehow struggling with the new shade of pink in her hair?

She pressed the speaker button. "What's going?"

A hologram popped up. "Your personal items are being boxed up," her supervisor said.

"What do you mean?"

"Apparently one of our most important heroes has decided to quit in order to pursue his dream of being a street photographer using, get this, a tablet. Not even a camera or even a phone. Like a Boomer."

"I don't understand," Rose said.

"You failed, Rose. I've been here for three decades and never once have I seen a simple help desk request lead to a hero quitting his job," her supervisor said.

"So, I'm fired?" Rose asked.

"Yes and no," her supervisor answered. "You're being transferred to hero training and development."

"Hero training and development?" Rose asked, her mind swimming with the gadgets she might use with emerging heroes.

"You're number one in the leader boards. You're solid gamer, a decent athlete, and an excellent engineer. According to our predictive analytics, you might just be successful. But not as an engineer," her supervisor said.

"So, I'm not fired?" Rose asked.

"You've been transferred to a new department. Let the A.I. make the decisions and you'll be fine," her supervisor said.

"I still don't understand," Rose said.

"Listen, Rose. You're our next hero," her supervisor said.

"But I'm not a hero," Rose protested.

"Not yet. But you will be. Just focus on actions. Use the automations. Let the A.I. make the decisions. It's been doing 87% of the work for him. He just didn't know it. Training begins in an hour. You'll be taking on his super suit. From this day forward, you are Swift Strike."

CHAPTER 5

WE CAN'T PREDICT HOW A.I. WILL CHANGE LEARNING

"What do you think all of this means for our kids?" a friend asks.

"I don't know," I answer.

"I mean, our kids are about to go to college. They're going to a choose a major and then what? Does the job they choose even exist in a decade?" he asks.

"I kind of feel like it won't. I mean, it might exist in name but it's going to look totally different. There are moments when that feels scary and other times it feels exciting and then there are these other times when I think maybe A.I. won't change things much at all," I say.

"I try to remind myself that this isn't even about A.I.," he adds, before taking a sip from his pint. "Our parents had the same worries. This is just what it means to have a senior who's about to go out on his own. When we went to college it wasn't A.I. It was something else but I'm sure it was something. The economy maybe? The threat of nuclear warfare? I have no idea what it was, but I know they felt the same things we feel right now."

We don't know how A.I. will change learning. We don't know how it will change thinking. We can't predict how it will change social, political, and economic systems. We simply don't know.

In the previous chapters, we explored the nature of A.I. and how we might respond to it. We examined the two dead ends of Techno Futurism and Lock It and Block It. We took a detour for a fictional short story that had nothing to do with teaching and A.I. and also everything to do with it. In this chapter, we'll focus on the unpredictability of A.I. and the reality that our roadmap will likely evolve in the upcoming years.

WE CAN'T PREDICT HOW A.I. WILL CHANGE THE WORLD

WE ARE IN A STAGE OF MORAL PANIC

Right now, A.I. feels scary because it's new. Collectively, we have a picture of artificial intelligence forged largely by fictional works like *Blade Runner, Battle Star Galactica,* and the *Terminator* franchise. If you're my age, you might have an image of high school troublemaker David in *WarGames* as well.

There's an uncanny humanness to the creative answers you receive with A.I. chatbots.

The knee-jerk reaction is often "how do I stop this?" But this isn't a new phenomenon.

Every time we experience a new technology, we also experience a moral panic. We hear dire warnings about what the technology will destroy and how our world will change. But this is often an overreaction.

Consider the humble bicycle. When the bike was invented, newspapers predicted everything from neurological diseases to distortions of the face (so-called "bicycle face") to psychological damage.[30] [31] Columnists warned of young women being addicted to bike-riding. When telephones were invented, citizens were concerned that the phones would explode.[32] People fought against telephone polls for fear that they would cause physical harm. But over time, the technology becomes boring.

You can think about it as a graph with time as the independent variable and concern as the dependent variable. You can imagine it like a graph with unawareness, moral panic, acceptance, and finally boredom.[33]

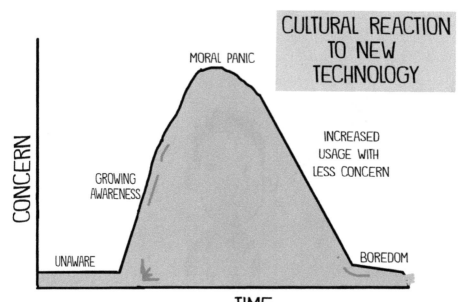

It starts with a general lack of awareness. In this phase, there's a mild concern based largely on the unknown. However, the technology is off in a distant future. But once we grow aware of this new technology, there's a resistance that builds into a moral panic. Here, the new technology is scary simply because it's new. We read reactionary articles about all the things this technology will destroy. Yet, as we adopt the emerging technology, the fear dissipates. We grow more comfortable with the technology as a part of our reality. Eventually, the technology grows so pervasive we hardly notice. It becomes boring.

I experienced this on a personal level with data tracking. I hated the notion that tech companies would know my location. But now I use an app to determine the location of my kids. What felt like an invasive app has now become commonplace.

THE DANGER
IS IN THE BORING
STAGE

HOW WE INTERACT

PRIVACY

DEMOCRACY

RELATIONSHIPS

CREATIVE
WORK

INFORMATION
LITERACY

CRIMINAL JUSTICE
AND PUBLIC
SAFETY

HOW WILL A.I. IMPACT
THE FOLLOWING?

While so much of the talk about generative AI
has been about cheating, here are some other
areas where AI might have huge unintended
consequences in our world.

CULTURAL
INTERACTIONS

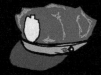

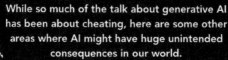

HEALTH CARE

TRANSPORTATION

THE JOB MARKET

THE WAY WE EAT

THE ENVIRONMENT

HOW WE LEARN

TECHNOLOGY IS MOST DANGEROUS WHEN IT IS BORING

Right now, we are at peak freak-out mode with A.I. Schools are wrestling with how to handle it. But someday it will be boring. And it's at this boring phase that we need to be most concerned. If the moral panic phase is an overreaction, the boredom phase is an under reaction. It's an uncritical acceptance of technology as the tools become more normalized and eventually invisible. It's a failure to grasp the way our tools are reshaping us because they seem so mundane. We forget that cars are powerful because we drive them all the time. They've become boring death machines.

A.I. will impact our social, political, and economic systems in ways we cannot predict. We will think and act differently. However, none of us can predict these changes to any degree of accuracy. Not social scientists. Not technologists. Not futurists. None of us. In a decade, we will all be surprised.

When the aforementioned bicycle was invented, few could have predicted how it would impact the women's suffrage movement.[34] Few could have seen the ways it would connect people and spark social movements between and within cities. Instead, people were worried about "bicycle face." No one could have predicted the way the Industrial Revolution would emphasize the nuclear family, change our self-perceptions, lead to a belief in personal privacy, and spark climate change.

Gutenberg could not have predicted how the printing press would lead to the rise of the nation-state and Enlightenment thinking.[35] Glass lens manufacturers had no idea that their work would eventually lead to telescopes, the scientific method, and the rise of secularism.

As we think about an earlier generation of A.I., people were largely concerned about "stranger danger" on social media. While that threat turned out to be somewhat overblown, few people predicted how it would impact social systems. We had no idea how strong the fear of missing out would be on youth mental health or the way it would lead to a rise of factionalism in filter bubbles.[36] We also had no idea how powerful it would be for telling stories, for making reconnecting with lost friends, for getting an opportunity to publish and build an audience without any gatekeepers.

Social media, like all technology, has its pros and cons. It's easy to look back and say, "How did we miss that?" But without a DeLorean and a flux capacitor, it is nearly impossible to predict the future.[37] A.I. will impact us in significant ways. We just don't know how. So, where do we go from here?

THINK CRITICALLY BUT THINK HUMBLY

The problem with asking, "How will A.I. change learning?" is it treats A.I. as if it's something in the distant future. However, A.I. has been around for decades. It has always impacted us. For this reason, it helps to ask students to think about A.I. in the present day.

Instead of asking students, "How will A.I. change society?" we should start with the question, "How is A.I. already changing your lives?" We can engage students in hard conversations about smart phones and attention spans — not from a curmudgeonly way so much as a curious way.

We are often poor predictors of the future and oblivious of the present. But the more we think critically in the present, the better we are at anticipating to the future. We might even ask students to engage in a Socratic Seminar about how A.I. is shaping their world. We'll explore this idea in-depth in Chapter 15 as we think about A.I. in social studies.

However, sometimes the best way to think critically about a big topic like A.I. is to explore it through the lens of fiction. At a younger grade, students might read a picture book like, *Robots, Robots, Everywhere*[38] or *Boy and Bot*.[39] These picture books can help launch a bigger discussion about the how smart machines work and what it means for our world.

With older students, we might use cyberpunk classics like *Do Androids Dream of Electric Sheep?*[40] or *Neuromancer.*[41] Students might examine the *Three Laws of Robotics* in Isaac Asimov's classic *I, Robot.*[42] For a take on Cinderella and the question about robot consciousness, students might enjoy the YA novel *Cinder* by Marissa Meyer.[43] One of my favorite fictional reads on A.I. is *Klara and the Sun* by Kazuo Ishiguro.[44] These novels can help students explore the nuances and complexities of artificial intelligence in our world.

INVITE STUDENTS INTO THE CONVERSATION

Ben Farrell is the Assistant Head of School / Director of the Upper School at the New England Innovation Academy. In early December of 2022, when students began using ChatGPT, he didn't create a schoolwide ban. He didn't accuse students of cheating. Instead, he asked questions and invited students into a dialogue about what it might mean to use A.I. in a way that's ethical and responsible.

As Farrell describes it, "It's crucial to empower them to have open discussions, and I feel strongly about that. In the conversation we had, I think a lot of wisdom emerged. We observed a range of opinions, like bumpers in a bowling alley. One student remarked that this could be the 'death of original thought,' expressing concern for the impact on creativity. On the other hand, some students wondered if we could use this technology for everything, questioning the need for traditional written papers. So, there's a spectrum of viewpoints to consider."[45]

From there, they worked together to define an actual policy for generative A.I. In the upcoming months, they plan to have more conversations and revise their policy as the technology evolves and the context changes.

While so many schools rushed to ban ChatGPT, Farrell asked students, "What does this mean for the future of your work? How does this impact your creative process?" Then, he listened.

As he describes it, "Students will inevitably discuss the topic elsewhere. If we can't facilitate such discussions in a school setting, I believe we're missing out on a valuable opportunity. Of course, different schools and school systems have their unique perspectives on this matter. However, if we can encourage and participate in these conversations, that's what's truly exciting and beneficial for everyone involved."

Note that this process is messy and chaotic. It's easier to try and craft a clear-cut policy for A.I. within a school. But a dialogue is more human – and ultimately more practical. If we can invite students into a conversation and listen with open minds, we are more likely to craft a solution that fits the needs of our students. The result is an adaptable policy that schools can modify as they learn more about the effects of A.I. on learning.

We don't know how A.I. will change learning. We can't predict how it will change our world, but we can ask hard questions about how technology is changing our world. We can encourage students to embrace all their imperfections and humbly recognize our shared humanity.

If we want to understand artificial intelligence, we are first going to need to understand ourselves. To do so, we will need to take a human-centered route through a world being transformed by machine learning. In the upcoming chapters, we will explore what it means to take this human-centered approach in a world where A.I. is transforming creativity, information, and learning.

PART TWO

HOW WILL
ARTIFICIAL INTELLIGENCE
CHANGE THE LANDSCAPE
OF LEARNING?

In Part One, we explored the basics of A.I. and how we, as educators, might respond to it. We examined the two dead ends we want to avoid as we move through our A.I. Roadmap. We recognized the sheer unpredictability of A.I. and how it will impact our world.

In this next section, we will explore the profound ways A.I. is changing the landscape of learning. We will go beyond just the role of generative A.I. and cheating (a legitimate concern) and into areas such as media literacy and creativity. We'll explore what it means to use these tools wisely from creative work, differentiated instruction, and personalized learning. We'll consider the ways we can use A.I. for authentic, student-centered assessments. We will explore how A.I. will create challenges and opportunities as our students engage in project-based learning. In other words, we will be analyzing how A.I. is changing the learning process in every domain.

So, let's continue this journey!

CHAPTER 6

REDEFINING
INFORMATION LITERACY
IN A WORLD OF A.I.

In 2014, Microsoft launched a hugely successful A.I. bot named Xiaoice in China.[46] With over forty million conversations, users often described feeling as though they were interacting with a real human. Microsoft founder Bill Gates described it this way, "'Xiaoice has attracted 45 million followers and is quite skilled at multitasking. And I've heard she's gotten good enough at sensing a user's emotional state that she can even help with relationship breakups."[47]

Xiaoice has published poetry, recorded musical albums, hosted television shows, and released audiobooks for children.[48] She's such a superstar that it's easy to forget she is merely a set of complex algorithms.

In 2016, Microsoft hoped to duplicate Xiaoice's success with the introduction of Tay in the U.S.A. This would be the virtual assistant of the future. Part influencer and part helper. Part content creator and part counselor. However, within hours, Tay began posting sexist and racist rants on Twitter.[49] [50] She spouted off unhinged conspiracy theories and engaged in trolling behaviors.

So, what happened? As trolls and bots spammed Tay with offensive content, the A.I. began to mimic racist and sexist speech.[51] As the bot attempted to "learn" how to interact with a community, it picked up on the mores and norms of a group that deliberately spammed it with racist and sexist content. By the time Microsoft shut Tay down, the bot had begun promoting Nazi ideology.

More recently, Microsoft has faced challenges with its Bing chatbot. When Associated Press report Matt O'Brien tested out the new A.I., the chatbot began complaining about news coverage. From there, it shifted to ad hominem personal attacks, calling O'Brien fat and ugly. Then it went into full-fledge internet trolling mode by comparing the reporter to Hitler.[52] On another occasion, the Bing chatbot claimed to fall in love with the reporter Sindhu Sundar. When he rejected the bot's advances, the Bing A.I. declared him an enemy.[53]

While this these are extreme examples, deeper learning machines will always contain biases. There's no such thing as a "neutral" A.I. because it pulls its data from the larger culture, and it will "learn" social norms and values from its vast data set.

It's easy to miss the subtler biases and the misinformation embedded within generative A.I. when it often produces accurate content. In some sense, ChatGPT poses a different challenge than Tay because the bias is less overt but still powerful.

And yet, when people interact with A.I. bots, they are more likely to assume that the information is unbiased and objective.[54] [55] I've already noticed people saying things like, "I treat ChatGPT like a search engine" or "AI can teach you pretty much anything."

In the upcoming decade, A.I. will fundamentally change the larger media landscape. Our students will inhabit a space where generative A.I. can create instant content that seems inherently human. They'll have to navigate a world of deepfakes and misinformation.

But this isn't a new phenomenon. A.I. has been changing the larger information landscape for decades. Before diving into deepfakes, let's explore how A.I. has already transformed the way we interact with media.

THE RISE OF FILTER BUBBLES

As social media platforms emerged in the early 2000s, computer scientists designed algorithms to focus on relevance. For the first time ever, users began to experience an entirely personalized media experience tailored to their ideas, beliefs, values, and preferences. At the same time, users could also create and share their own content without the need for official gatekeepers. Combined with the advent of new media technology (like podcasting and blogging), the media landscape shifted from one of broadcasting to narrowcasting.[56]

With this democratization of media, it was easier than ever to create, edit, and publish one's work to the world. Voices that had previously been excluded found a place online to share their ideas and insights. People without formal journalistic training could now set up a blog and share their ideas on topics that might not appeal to everyone.

With so much information and a lack of official gatekeepers, algorithms functioned like gatekeepers by prioritizing media based on relevance. For the last two decades, children have grown up with a worldview shaped as much by A.I. as by geography. This has created some phenomenal learning opportunities in a connected world. However, relevance-based algorithms have also led to filter bubbles and echo chambers.[57]

Filter bubbles refer to the phenomenon where individuals are increasingly exposed to customized content that reinforces their existing beliefs, values, and preferences while excluding contradictory information. This means a progressive Green party member who focuses on ecological justice gets increasingly left-leaning content while a libertarian Conservative party member has an entirely different media experience that skews conservative.

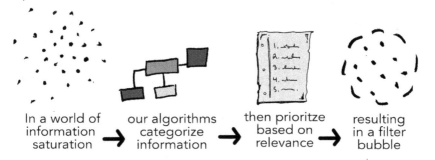

In a world of information saturation → our algorithms categorize information → then prioritze based on relevance → resulting in a filter bubble

People grow more polarized in their views as they are exposed to information that confirms their biases and are less likely to encounter information that challenges their beliefs. This results in an echo chamber, where people remain insulted from outside perspectives and simply listen to other voices that echo their beliefs. People in an echo chamber can't hear alternative viewpoints. which ultimately hinders one's ability to make informed decisions and engage in meaningful discourse.

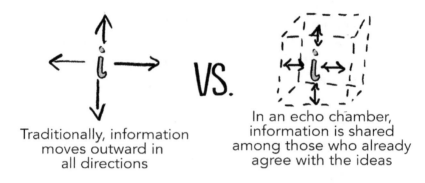

Traditionally, information moves outward in all directions

In an echo chamber, information is shared among those who already agree with the ideas

Filter bubbles and echo chambers work in part by clicks and "likes." But these are often manipulated using A.I. bots. Typically, bots have used simple algorithms or scripts to create a signal boost on certain ideas or to attack members of a different group or ideology. But with generative A.I., there's a very real concern about the human-like quality of this newer type of bot. Microsoft shut down Tay when she spewed Nazi rhetoric but what happens when people engineer bots to emphasize totalitarian rhetoric or to promote racist ideology?

With generative A.I., bots can mimic the style of an actual user. This creates huge concerns for misinformation and catfishing (which we'll address later in this chapter). It's easy to imagine how an army of generative A.I. bots could potentially manipulate public opinion by crafting text with a tone of credibility or engaging in conversational tactics meant to manipulate the larger population.

Part of how we develop our beliefs is by interacting with one another. This is especially true of our students, who are often trying to make sense of their world. With generative A.I., these bots won't simply like or retweet a post. They'll engage in a full conversation in a tone that can show a range of emotions – from authentic to authoritative to approachable.

Despite the age limits on social media, many elementary teachers have noticed that children in the third or fourth grade already have access to social media on their own smart phones. And many earlier gaming programs, aimed at younger students, use social media elements within their platforms.

Our students are growing up in an information ecosystem shaped by A.I. and traditional approaches to information literacy might not be enough for them to navigate this new landscape.

THE RISE OF MISINFORMATION

Right after the Super Bowl in 2023, my son texted me about Patrick Mahomes failing a drug test during Halftime. Two other friends texted me memes relating to this. Three friends posted this to Twitter. A few hours later, I looked at multiple news sources and learned that this had been a hoax. It turned out that Mahomes was simply an elite quarterback and Andy Reid was a phenomenal coach.

Interestingly, my friends who spread this hoax were not typically gullible. One was a technology director who had taught professional development sessions on media literacy. One was a journalism teacher. Another was a language arts teacher. None of them were the types to send chain letters or buy into wild conspiracies.

However, I've been guilty of sharing misinformation as well. I once shared an article that I thought was from ABC News until a former student of mine messaged me on Facebook and said, "Mr. Spencer, you need to follow the advice you gave us. Look at the URL first. That's not ABC News. It's a spoofing site." I was so embarrassed!

Currently, it's easier than ever to spread misinformation. According to a Pew Research Center right after the 2016 election, roughly 64% of adults believed that fake news stories caused a significant level of confusion. What's more, 23% of respondents admitted to sharing political stories that were totally made up, either by accident or on purpose.[58]

We see similar trends with students. According to a Stanford study, only 25% of high school students were able to identify an accurate news story when also given a fake one. Students also had a hard time distinguishing between real and fake photographs as well as authentic and staged videos. Researchers used the words "bleak" and "dismaying" to describe it.[59] But it's not going away anytime soon.[60] With generative A.I., it's becoming easier for bad actors to create and spread misinformation.

One example is the rise of the deep fake. The term "deepfake" is a combination of "deep learning" and "fake."[61] It's essentially an A.I.-generated video or audio clip that has been manipulated to make it look like someone has said something they never said.

Deepfakes use machine learning techniques to identify and replicate the nuances of a person's voice, facial expressions, and movements.[62] The goal is to create convincing videos or audio clips. These are often imperfect. In the case of video, you can usually sense that something is off. But they are getting more accurate with each new iteration.

With deep fakes, it's easy to spread disinformation, defame individuals, and create false news stories. A deepfake video of a politician making inflammatory comments could be used to discredit their reputation or sway public opinion. This could be huge when coupled with filter bubbles and echo chambers. On a more individual level, deep fakes can play a profound role in catfishing and extortion schemes.

DEEP FAKES AND THE ELIZA EFFECT

Back in Chapter 1, I mentioned the Turing test. The Turing Test is a concept introduced by the British mathematician Alan Turing in 1950. During the test, a human judge engages in a conversation with two participants, one human and the other an A.I. program, without knowing which is which. If the judge is unable to reliably distinguish between the two, the A.I. is considered to have passed the test.

What's fascinating is just how easily humans can be duped by machines. Part of this is due to innate pattern recognition. We have a natural cognitive bias toward finding patterns and attributing causality even when the data is random.[63] When an A.I. produces responses that resemble human communication, our brains recognize the patterns and can be convinced that there's a human behind the interaction. It just feels more human. Moreover, humans tend to have a default toward trust.[64]

This trust is amplified through the ELIZA Effect, where people attribute human-like intelligence and emotions to computer programs, even when they know the responses are generated by simple algorithms. This phenomenon is named after ELIZA, an early A.I. program developed in the 1960s by Joseph Weizenbaum at MIT. Despite the program's limited capabilities, users often formed emotional connections with ELIZA and attributed understanding and empathy to the program. The ELIZA Effect highlights our tendency to anthropomorphize technology and perceive more intelligence in A.I. systems than may be present. In the case of ELIZA, people knew it was a machine. But what happens when they can't distinguish between human and machine online?

THE DANGERS OF CATFISHING

A.I.-generated deepfakes can have devastating impact on vulnerable people when used for catfishing. Catfishing occurs when someone creates a fake account and uses that to lure in a victim.

Dr. Alec Couros has dealt with victims of catfishing after criminals used his photos as part of scams.[65] To be clear, he had nothing to do with the scams. Criminals had used his online photos in their fake accounts. They then found victims online who they pulled in through romance scams. Victims lost thousands of dollars, sometimes through blackmail and sometimes through false promises.

Dr. Couros has shared his concerns about the more sophisticated approach to catfishing in an era of deepfakes. He describes it this way, "I've spent a lot of time learning about catfishing firsthand. But now at this point we have generative A.I. that can pick up style and tone. You can use something like Descript which is a really powerful tool. If you speak to it for 10 minutes, it will pick up your audio. It will mimic your voice and you can create any script you want and it will create the audio in your voice." [66]

As deepfakes grow more sophisticated and chatbots become more human in their tone, catfishing will become harder to root out. In recent times, there has been a rise in catfishing aimed at young boys, who share intimate pictures with a stranger spoofing a friend's account. From there, the catfishers use bullying, threats, and extortion to gain access to their loved one's banking information. Criminals often create deepfakes of the victims themselves and threaten to send those to the child's parents. The frightened child, who hasn't post anything inappropriate feels trapped.

This will only accelerate as deepfakes grow more realistic. As Couros points out, "Down the road, there will be a more powerful tool. So you've got voice. You've got style. You've got video. In terms of catfishing, you've got everything that you possibly need to fool people - whether it's on a personal front if it's something political."

So, where do we go from here? How do we help our students determine what is real in a world of disinformation and deepfakes? How do you keep them protected from generative A.I. catfishing schemes? How do you help them seek out new ideas and opinions when they're surrounded by an echo chamber? How can they discover truth in the world when there's so much misinformation?

Traditional approaches to informational literacy aren't enough. We need new approaches. One place to start is lateral reading.

THE VALUE OF LATERAL READING

Mike Caulfield, the Director of Blended and Networked Learning at Washington State University Vancouver, coined the term "lateral reading" in 2017.[67] [68] Caulfield recognized that older inform literacy models weren't realistic in today's fast-paced, hyper-connected landscape. Consider the CRAAP Test. It's an easy acronym to remember. It stands for Currency, Relevance, Authority, Accuracy, and Purpose (2004). Caulfield believes it doesn't capture the reality of how people read online.[69]

He describes it this way, "Checklist approaches like the CRAAP test actually come out of old library collection development criteria.[70] They are the questions you would ask as a librarian when deciding whether to purchase a book or journal for your library collection. Over time those questions have been refined to create a student tool for thinking about documents. But it's never really worked online. When we're online nowadays we are the filter.[71]"

In other words, these information literacy tools (often checklists) weren't designed to handle so much misinformation and fake news. Instead of using a checklist to go through a single source, students might need to engage in what Caulfield called "lateral reading." Lateral reading is a more dynamic approach to fact-checking. Caulfield argued that traditional fact-checking methods, such as verifying a source's credibility before reading its contents, are not effective. Instead, he advocated for a "looking sideways" approach that involves examining the context in which information is shared. Context is key here.

To go beyond surface-level information and get a better understanding of a source, lateral reading is key. This involves examining the context in which the information was created, such as the author's background and potential biases, the publication or website's reputation, and the wider social and political landscape.

To practice lateral reading, you might start by conducting research on the author or publisher of the original source to determine their credibility. This could include checking their credentials, affiliations, and track record to ensure that they are a trustworthy source of information. Additionally, you could investigate the publication or website where the information was first shared to determine its reliability.

Next, seek out alternative viewpoints and additional sources of information to help you evaluate the original source. This might involve reading articles from different news outlets or using fact-checking websites to determine if the information presented in the original source is accurate and well-supported.

At this point, a student finally considers credibility. This includes considering the author's motives, the reliability of the information presented, and the broader social and political context in which the information is being shared. By engaging in lateral reading, you can develop a more nuanced understanding of complex issues and avoid being misled by misinformation.

The challenge with vertical reading is that students go through a long process with a single website. But the sheer complexity can create a certain tunnel vision. As Jennifer A. Fielding describes it, "in recent years the dissemination of mis- and disinformation online has become increasingly sophisticated and prolific, so restricting analysis to a single website's content without understanding how the site relates to a wider scope now has the potential to facilitate the acceptance of misinformation as fact."[72]

Caulfield has developed what he calls the SIFT Method as an alternative to the CRAAP Test.[73] It's an acronym that stands for Stop, Investigate, Find better coverage, and Trace Claims. Here's how it works:

The four steps of the SIFT method are:
1. **Stop:** Before engaging with the information, take a moment to assess your emotional response and consider the motivations of the person or organization that shared the information.
2. **Investigate the Source**: Evaluate the credibility of the source of the information, including the author, publisher, and

website. Look for signs of bias, conflicts of interest, and expertise in the topic.

3. **Find Trusted Coverage:** Verify the accuracy of the information by finding multiple sources that corroborate the claims. Look for reliable news sources and fact-checking websites.

4. **Trace Claims, Quotes, and Media Back to the Original Context:** Follow the information back to its original source, including any quotes or media used to support the claims. Look for any misrepresentations or distortions of the information.

By following the SIFT method, readers can develop a critical understanding of the information they encounter online and make informed decisions about its credibility and accuracy.

However, lateral reading might not be enough in a world of A.I. Information literacy expert Jennifer LaGarde has pointed out that lateral reading doesn't take into consideration the emotional aspects of reading. We often buy into fake information and deep fakes because of the way this content makes us feel.

Lateral reading assumes students will engage in media literacy on laptops while doing online research. However, that doesn't capture the way students often consume media. Students scroll through social media, quickly reading articles, looking at memes, watching videos, and engaging in rapid-fire conversations on a smartphone. In other words, lateral reading doesn't fit the typical way we process digital information on our smartphones. LaGarde points out that most of our students view content on mobile devices in a fast, informal, media consumption mode. In other words, they're not using acronyms or checklists.

NOBODY SCROLLS THROUGH SOCIAL MEDIA HOLDING A CHECKLIST

INFORMATION LITERACY IS AS MUCH

A MINDSET

AND A HABIT

AS IT IS A SKILL

TREATING INFORMATION LITERACY AS A MINDSET

After my son realized he had fallen for the fake story about Patrick Mahomes, he admitted, "That's not like me to fall for that type of fake news."

I then asked what he thought about SIFT and CRAAP and he said, "I like lateral thinking. It's what we've learned in school. But we also take elements of the CRAAP test. We start by thinking laterally but then when you decide a source seems credible, you do a deep dive where you keep things like relevance, accuracy, bias, and purpose. It might be a great site but if you realize they're trying to sell you something, the purpose has changed."

But then he said, "Dad, you know that's not really what people do most of the time, though."

"They don't use lateral reading?" I asked.

"Not really. Some of the most dangerous viral misinformation is on social media. People aren't pulling up Wikipedia to see the multiple sources connected to what they read. They're not doing a Google Search. They're scrolling until they find something interesting."

"So, what do people actually do?" I asked.

"I can't speak for others. But for me, I start out as a skeptic. If something seems too strange, too incredible, too good to be true. Whatever. You stop and doublecheck," he said.

"What do you look at when you doublecheck things?"

"I look at the profile. Is it a meme page? That's probably not accurate. Is it a news source? Okay, I'm doublechecking that it's verified. I'm going to my browser and then checking other sources. Sometimes, I look at the number of followers. Famous people usually have millions of followers, not thousands."

"So, social proof?" I ask.

"Yeah, the social proof. But also the username. Bots usually have crappy usernames. The fakes are usually obvious. Then you look at the comments. If it's not a real account, there's always a group of people ready to explain why. They call it out in the comment section."

"So, it really is all about the trustworthiness of the person?" I ask.

"Yeah. And just because someone is famous doesn't mean we can trust their expertise. You might have a famous actor or entrepreneur or athlete who has a big audience but doesn't know anything about science, for example. You have to be a skeptic."

From there, he went on to describe how he notices misinformation in deep fakes and altered images. There are the typical tells. The voice seems a little off. The footage is grainy. The video has a strange mashup quality. But the biggest factor is the question, "Could this really have happened?" If the answer is "no" or even "I'm not sure," it's a moment to investigate. He might go to different credible websites but he might look into Reddit. While Reddit isn't exactly the most reliable source, he's found smaller subreddits that do a great job at fact-checking. As he described it, "You can go to Snopes. However, if it what was just published, Snopes is going to be behind. You have to ask around."

As he describes this process, I'm struck by how dependent it is on people. Read the comments. Check a subreddit. Ask around before you share. It's not a checklist. It's a conversation. It's a messy process that doesn't resemble a checklist.

I'm not sure what to think about this. There's a danger in choosing the wrong community and following a herd mentality. But there's also a value in the human dynamic of looking at perspectives and thinking critically about what people say rather than using a checklist or heuristic.

I'm also struck by the overall stance of skepticism. If something seems too "out there," it's a red flag that he then explores. My son is going to scroll. He's going to move through Reels and Posts at breakneck speed. But he does so skeptically.

The future of information literacy needs to be more than just a set of skills. Students will need to adopt it as a mindset and continue it as a habit. Jennifer LaGarde and Darren Hudgins use the metaphor of a digital detective to describe this mindset.[74]

1. **The Triggers Lens:** Digital Detectives use this lens to make sense out of the ways information elicit an emotional response.
2. **The Access Lens:** Digital Detectives use this lens to see how platforms and devices determine what is a credible source. For example, a news story looks different on a mobile device than on a browser. It's also a chance to think about how the community impacts interpretations of information. So, the way people on Twitter and Facebook interact with a news story will vary.
3. **The Forensics Lens:** This is the lens that we tend to think of as information literacy. Here is where students investigate the information from a place of curiosity.
4. **The Motives Lens:** This is where students think about the motives of those who are creating misinformation. Like any great detective, they consider why people might manipulate information.

LaGarde and Hudgins argue that the solution goes beyond simply developing a set of information literacy skills. Instead, students need to develop these mindsets in conjunction with the broader SEL Competencies of Self-Awareness, Self-Management, Social Awareness, Relationship Skills, and Responsible Decision-Making.

The Digital Detectives approach recognizes the distinction between informal information literacy and formal information literacy. We tend to read informally and formally, perusing articles for fun and doing close reading when it's highly academic. We tend to write in formal and informal registers. A text message contains poop emojis. An essay contains complex sentences and citations.

Similarly, students need to use different information literacy approaches based on the type of device they're using and their purpose of their information consumption. If we treat information literacy only as a skill for doing academic research (think lateral reading) for things like Instagram posts, our students fail to develop the informal information literacy they will need in an information landscape dominated by A.I.

SEEK OUT LIBRARIANS

The media landscape has been changing for the last three decades and it will continue to transform in ways that we can't even predict. The newest forms of A.I. present huge challenges with deepfakes, catfishing, and misinformation. We cannot rely entirely on older tools like the CRAAP test, and we cannot assume that students will use an academic approach similar to lateral reading every time they consume content. Information literacy will not only need to be a skill. It will need to be a habit and a mindset of critical thinking and adaptability. The approaches we use will change as the landscape continues to change.

Librarians are more important than ever. We cannot lean into a single model or process for information and media literacy. Our students will need to learn these skills in a dynamic and human way. Schools need to tap into the expertise of librarians in helping students learn this newer type of information literacy and develop it as a mindset rather than just a skill.

I recently engaged in a conversation about generative A.I. with a group of educators in Connecticut. The school was wrestling with the opportunities and challenges of ChatGPT. At one point, the librarian said something that stuck with me.

"We need to change the Works Cited approach. We call it Works Cited but it's just a throwback to a bibliography. But what if we treated it as a journey? What if we organized it chronologically as a story? And in terms of sources, it might involve talking to experts, looking at exemplars, or hashing things out with classmates. But it might also include A.I. And if it's a story, we get a bigger picture of their research process."

She was asking the hard questions about the changing information landscape and had a vision for changing their works cited process on their essays and projects.

As A.I. systems generate more content, it becomes increasingly challenging for individuals to determine the credibility and relevance of the information they encounter. Librarians are experts in evaluating, organizing, and providing access to reliable resources, ensuring that people can access trustworthy information and make well-informed decisions.

Note that they are not gatekeepers so much as guides who teach students to think critically about the media they encounter. By empowering students with these skills, librarians help them become responsible digital citizens who can think critically about what they consume.

When I think of A.I., I am less concerned about cheating or Skynet taking over the world or even everyone losing their jobs and more concerned about deepfakes and catfishing. But my hope is that by developing information literacy as both a skill and a mindset, we can help students navigate the everchanging information landscape.

CHAPTER 7
REDEFINING CREATIVE THINKING IN A WORLD OF A.I.

I open the refrigerator and stare into the void. Nothing sounds good. I want something spicy and different and healthy. Oh, yeah, and easy to make.

I pull out my laptop and go to ChatGPT, where I type in the following prompt, "I have lettuce, ground beef, Greek yogurt, and eggs. What is a lunch I could make with it? I want it to be spicy. I have most seasonings in the cupboard."

I reject the first idea. It's a spicy lettuce wrap with a side of scrambled eggs. Nope. I don't like lettuce wraps. I feel like the food always crumbles and spills out. Just skip the wrap and make it a salad. I refresh the A.I. The next idea is better. It's a spicy devilled egg salad. Unfortunately, it feels like too much work. So, I change up the ingredients. This time, the ingredients are eggs, a tortilla, shredded chicken, buffalo sauce, and Greek yogurt.

It looks decent, but I'm not sure how much to add of each ingredient. I ask ChatGPT to modify the recipe to include a few more spices and to give me precise measurements. It works. I end up with a step-by-step recipe. I then ask it to estimate the time it will take. Fifteen minutes. That's perfect. How about the macros? The chatbot gives me an estimation that I then modify on my own. The result is a Buffalo chicken wrap that tastes amazing.

For the last six months, I have been using ChatGPT as a modified version of the television show *Chopped!* Give it some random ingredients and see what it comes up with. Sometimes I ask for certain flavor profiles. Sometimes I add time constraints for prepping and cooking. But I've been impressed with the creative thinking.

And yet, if I tried to pass off any of these recipes on the show *Chopped!*, I doubt they would win. Most of the recipes are a bit derivative. They lack the deeper divergent thinking you get from master chefs who regularly push the envelope. Still, it's an example of how this newer form of generative A.I. will redefine creative work in the future.

In fact, chefs are already using machine learning as a part of their research and development process.[75] Food scientists use A.I. to develop new recipes by analyzing a large dataset of existing recipes and generating new combinations of ingredients and cooking techniques.[76] They also use A.I. to optimize menus based on consumer feedback.[77] A.I. can analyze individual customer data for dietary preferences, allergies, and flavor profiles to create custom menus for special events.

Meanwhile, restaurants use A.I. services to optimize ingredient selection. A seemingly rustic farm-to-table restaurant might just use an A.I. system to predict weather patterns and climate variables to decide the optimal times to select certain local ingredients.

So, where does that leave the human element? At the end of the day, robots can't eat. They consume vast amounts of data but they can't tell you what it's like to see a dish for the first time and feel blown away by the presentation. They can't lean into a hunch and run with a new flavor profile that surprises loyal patrons. They can't experience food with all five senses. They can't take a bite of a brand-new dish and say, "This surprised me. French toast, anise, and a burger? I didn't think it would work, but wow." Just to clarify, this is entirely fictional. Please don't make a licorice French toast burger at home.

THE IMPORTANCE OF STUDENT VOICE

Earlier we explored how students will need to be really good at what A.I. can do and different with what A.I. can do. This is especially true in the everchanging landscape of creative work.

Our students will need to develop those skills that can't be replaced by a machine. But they'll also need to find innovative ways to do the things that machines *can* do. Instead of competing with A.I., our students will need to forge their own path. A.I. is great at synthesizing information but it's not great with voice. So, in writing, voice becomes more important than ever.

IN A WORLD OF A.I., STUDENT VOICE WILL BE MORE IMPORTANT THAN EVER

THINK OF IT LIKE
ICE CREAM

A.I. can give you vanilla and maybe chocolate or even strawberry. But it doesn't produce that salted caramel truffle or the campfire s'more ice cream that nobody knew they wanted until you made it. In the future, students will have an advantage if they can take the vanilla and then make it their own by adding those deeply human elements that automation can't replace - things like empathy, context, divergent thinking, and humor.

MOVING PAST VANILLA

Yesterday, I took one of my most popular writing prompts and plugged it into the A.I. The answer I got was solid but boring. But what if I used this as a starting place? I could start with the vanilla and add my own to make it more creative and perhaps even slightly funnier. **My revisions are in bold.** The prompt was, "Create a to do list for a supervillain."

1. Take over the world. **But maybe start out small. Perhaps an exoplanet? Or just take over Fresno. I'm not sure anyone will even notice.**
2. Steal the moon. **I mean, not our moon, of course. I need the moon if I'm going to keep surfing. I'm thinking maybe Titan or Io? Perhaps Callisto? Nobody ever pays attention to Callisto.**
3. Create a **shrink** ray **but one that only makes clothes shrink so that everyone in Fresno thinks they gained ten pounds overnight.**
4. Build a giant robot **navy. All the villains do an army. That's too cliché. We're going with a solid robot navy.**
5. Train army of **moderately sized** genetically-engineered **hamsters. Anything bigger will be unmanageable.**
6. Hijack Santa's sleigh and replace all the presents with **leftover recalled toys from the 1980s. How about lawn darts?**

7. Create a secret underground lair with a **moat full of that weird Midwestern Jell-O Salad that you're grandma used to make with the coconut and walnuts. While we are at it, let's replace the carpet with hardwood floors. Maybe the Property Brothers have some ideas?**

8. Come up with a ridiculous and over-the-top villainous name like **Kyle.**

9. Brainwash all the puppies in the world (they make great henchmen) **so that they act like cats and their owners can experience the rejection normally dished out by their feline companions**

10. Build a time machine and go back in time to **raise baby Batman to be a healthy, well-adjusted adult without any chip on his shoulder. Then attack Gotham City. They'll be defenseless without the Caped Crusader.**

I look at this new list. It's still heavily shaped by A.I. That's the vanilla. But this initial set of ideas led to a creative constraint. I had to think outside the box by thinking inside the box. The result was something more creative than what I would have written on my own.

While I began with A.I., I quickly focused on the things I can do: adding my own voice, having a touch of my quirky humor, and making a personal reference to where I grew up (Fresno). If we go back to that idea of a vintage innovation approach, I used the A.I. but ultimately added something human. Was it better? Depends on who you ask. Was it me? You bet.

This exercise was admittedly silly. However, it illustrates the approach our students will need to use. In a world of A.I., they'll need to tap into the speed and efficiency of machine learning, but they'll also need to engage in something slower and messier. They'll take the vanilla and create their own unique flavor (an idea we'll explore in Chapter 13).

WE ARE ALL COLLAGE ARTISTS

I can see how writers might use A.I. chatbots as a part of their process. They'll take the initial 300 words of a chatbot and rework it, add to it, find their own ideas, and ultimately make it their own. In that sense, writing will be more like collage art — which, in many respects, it already is.

Your solitary voice is distinctly yours but it's also part of a chorus shaped by the media you consume. It's shaped by the invisible hand of your culture. When you write, you are never writing alone. You are writing out of a set of social experiences. Generative A.I. won't erase human creativity. It will be another way that we tap into the existing culture and then add our own unique voice.

In a world of A.I., it is more important than ever that students consume content in an intentional way. We often hear the distinction between creativity and consuming as if these two acts are diametrically opposed. It's the idea that we should spend our time making rather than taking.

However, creativity doesn't happen in a vacuum. Chefs love great meals. Musicians listen to music. Architects often visit new cities and tour buildings to find inspiration. Filmmakers watch videos. Engineers often study objects within their world. Computer scientists view other people's lines of code. In other words, creative types consume what they love. There's often this ongoing cycle that starts with critical consuming and leads to creativity. See the diagram to the right.

CRITICAL CONSUMING

INSPIRATION

CREATIVE WORK

Critical consuming is intentional and mindful.[78] Here, you ask questions and seek out ideas. This leads to inspiration. You might mash-up multiple ideas or take a different angle to a problem. Often, you plan and design. But sometimes you play and experiment. This, in turn, leads to creative work. The more you create, the better you understand your craft, which leads to a deeper ability to consume critically, where you find more inspiration, and the cycle continues.

So, what can we do as educators? It starts by exposing students to a wide range of texts, concepts, viewpoints, and media. The goal here is range. If students are engaging in research, you might not start with a search engine and instead opt for a carefully curated set of resources that students can choose from. Thus, you introduce students to new ideas that challenge their thinking.

I love the way Ira Glass puts this, "Nobody tells this to people who are beginners, I wish someone told me. All of us who do creative work, we get into it because we have good taste. But there is this gap. For the first couple years you make stuff, it's just not that good. It's trying to be good, it has potential, but it's not. But your taste, the thing that got you into the game, is still killer. And your taste is why your work disappoints you."[79]

As students move through this critical consuming process, they become better curators. Here they ask thoughtful questions and find resources that are accurate and interesting. They geek out on the content; finding the takeaways and making sense out of ideas. As this happens, curators organize content into categories. They make connections between seemingly opposite artists, ideas, or disciplines in ways that make you think, "Wow, I never considered that before." They're also able to determine trends from multiple sources. They add their own unique lens that they share with an audience. This curation process ultimately inspires creative thinking.

Bringing this back to A.I., students will need to be great curators of information, ideas, and products. They'll need to have what Ira Glass describes as "killer taste." They'll need to determine whether the A.I.-generated work is worth modifying and making their own. They'll also need to know how to create the right types of command prompts so that the A.I. can take their original vision and turn it into something tangible that they can then revise. In this sense, A.I. functions like an exemplar generator that inspires creative thinking.

WHAT ABOUT COPYRIGHT?

Critics are rightfully worried about what generative A.I. means for copyright.[80] Generative A.I. mines vast swaths of data to design its own images. But what if the original artist didn't consent? Is this similar to an artist visiting several museums and then generating an entirely new work based on multiple artists? Or is this more like a singer who has sampled an artist's work in a new song (and thus would need to gain permission and pay mechanical royalties)? The answer is unclear.

Currently, A.I.-generated creative work cannot be copyrighted in most nations.[81] For example, the US. Copyright Office has stated they will "refuse to register a claim if it determines that a human being did not create the work." Furthermore, they will exclude any works "produced by machine or mere mechanical process that operates randomly or automatically without any creative input or intervention from a human author."[82]

And yet, what if the work has been significantly modified? What if, for example, someone sketches an original picture, then uses A.I. to generate a new picture in that style? Can the artist own the copyright of the new image? What if a writer uses A.I. to generate a text and then modifies the text with her own voice?

This is uncharted territory as we craft our A.I. roadmap. For now, we can encourage students to be transparent about when and how they borrow ideas. We can teach them to cite sources, not merely as a formal documentation in APA format, but as a part of the creative process. It might be as simple as saying, "I was influenced by the works of _____ " as an element they include when they turn in their work. We could follow the advice of the previously mentioned librarian who suggested that we treat works cited as a journey and where we all provide attribution to the larger network of ideas in our culture and community.

HOW ARE PEOPLE ALREADY USING A.I. IN CREATIVE WORK?

If we want to make sense out of the changing landscape of creative thinking, we might need to talk to the makers, engineers, artists, and other creative thinkers in the larger community.

If you're wondering, "How will generative A.I. change creative work in the future?" a great starting place would be to explore the ways it is currently changing creativity in the here and now. Here are a few examples.

1. **Music Composition:** A.I. algorithms can analyze existing music and generate new pieces based on those patterns. A.I.-powered music composition tools can also help musicians in creating melodies, harmonies, and chords for their music. A songwriter might use these tools as a vanilla starting place that they modify to craft a unique song.

2. **Image and Video Editing:** A.I.-powered tools can analyze and enhance images and videos, remove background noise, and even create 3D models from 2D images. In graphic design, A.I. can be used to create logos, designs, and other visual elements. A.I.-powered design tools can also help designers to automatically generate layout options, color schemes, and other design elements.

3. **Writing:** A.I. can help writers generate ideas, provide suggestions for sentence structure and grammar, and even write entire articles or stories based on specific guidelines.

4. **Gaming:** A.I. can be used to create more intelligent and adaptive games, allowing for more complex gameplay and scenarios.

5. **Finding Trends:** A.I. can analyze trends and consumer preferences to generate new designs that are more likely to be successful. So, a fashion designer might use A.I. to determine

new trends in clothing design and a large motion picture company might use A.I. to try and predict which movies might become hits.

6. **Product Design:** A.I. can help designers to create and test new product designs, optimizing for various factors such as cost, performance, and usability.

7. **Data Analysis and Prediction:** A.I. is being used to analyze large datasets and make predictions based on patterns identified in the data. For example, scientists might use machine learning algorithms can analyze complex biological data sets to identify potential drug targets for disease treatment.

8. **Optimization:** A.I. is being used to optimize complex processes, such as energy systems, manufacturing methods, and transportation systems. A.I. algorithms can help identify the optimal settings for a system, maximizing its efficiency and reducing waste.

9. **Simulation:** A.I. is being used to simulate complex systems, such as aircraft, cars, and buildings. A.I. algorithms can optimize designs and simulate their behavior in different conditions, allowing engineers to identify potential issues before building physical prototypes.

10. **Robotics:** A.I. is being used to develop autonomous robots that can perform tasks in environments that are hazardous or difficult for humans. For example, robots equipped with A.I. algorithms can perform tasks such as inspecting pipelines, exploring space, and delivering packages.

A.I. HAS THE ABILITY TO MAKE CREATIVE WORK

FASTER

AND CHEAPER

SAVING TIME AND MONEY

When I was in the eighth grade, I spent an entire year working on a slide presentation. I visited the library, explored the card catalogs, and found articles using microfilm and microfiche. I handwrote draft after draft of the script before eventually typing a first draft. I wrote notes in the margins and retyped the entire thing. When I interviewed former baseball players, I had to count the minutes because long distance phone calls were expensive. When I eventually had to create a bibliography, I looked up the APA process in a book and spent hours typing up the references. As I moved into the actual slide presentation, I found pictures in books and used a physical camera to snap a photo. Once I filled up the entire roll of film, I could then take it to the drug store to be developed hoping none of the slides were blurry. When I recorded my voice, I had to use massive reel-to-real magnetic tape and splice it using a razor blade and tape.

Everything was slow and expensive.

Fast forward three decades. I knock out a single slideshow in a few hours. I can find images online, but I typically sketch things out by hand. I don't have to wait a week for slides to develop at a drug store. I create sketch videos with my own voice and animations. No splicing necessary. I record and edit everything on GarageBand. When I talk to experts, I don't pay for long distance. I do video conferences using Zoom. When I want to read journal articles, I hop onto Google Scholar and search. I can't think of the last time I had to navigate the dark art of microfilm.

As a writer, podcaster, and video creator, I get to create content that I never dreamed I'd be able to do when I was in high school. I do all of this from the comfort of a 13x14 square foot studio. Technology has saved me time on the drudgery of certain creative tasks and freed me up to do the creative work I want to do.

A.I. has the potential to do the same. A.J. Juliani puts it this way, "This is where Artificial Intelligence can be such a tool for facilitating learning. It is the perfect learning partner and guide for creative work."[83] He shares a simple example of this:

- Need help writing a script or opening for a podcast/video? ChatGPT can help with that.
- Need creative ideas around color schemes and visuals for your project? DALL-E can help with that.
- Need to spend more time on making the podcast/video and less time on the audio cleanup? Cleanvoice.ai can help with that.
- Need background music to add to your podcast or video? Beatoven.ai can help with that.

Notice how students can still write their own scripts, film their own videos, and record their own podcasts. But A.I. can reduce the amount of time spent on the more tedious aspects of this creative work. As a former middle school teacher, this excites me. My students used to spend hours editing our documentaries. If an A.I. assistant could speed up the editing process, that would be a game changer.

Again, Juliani describes this process, "This type of learning assistant can help students cut through the noise, and focus on the making, creating, and designing parts of the learning experience. It also cuts down on the *time* needed to do creative work in our classrooms." This could be huge for project-based learning, which we will be exploring in our next chapter.

CHAPTER 8

REDEFINING
PROJECT-BASED LEARNING
IN A WORLD OF A.I.

Ricardo was a shy student. If I called on him, he would freeze up entirely. I wanted Ricardo to find his voice and build confidence. However, it wasn't working during direct instruction and guided practice, no matter how many scaffolds I provided. Instead, he had a breakthrough during an independent project.

Each student completed a Geek Out Blog and Ricardo chose engineering and robotics as his topic. At the end of the project, students had to share their geeky interests with the classmates. I offered students the chance to record and edit videos instead of doing a synchronous presentation. All they had to do was press "play" and let the projector do its job. This prerecorded process blended the high-stakes element of launching to an audience with the low-stakes opportunity to make mistakes and revise their work.

Ricardo didn't finish his video on time. For an entire week, I asked him if he was ready to present and he would smile slightly and say, "not yet." Eventually, it became a joke. He would walk into class and say, "not yet" before I could ask. But finally, three weeks later, he walked in with a jump drive.

"It's ready," he said.

Ricardo's video was well-produced, with creativity and humor infused throughout the entire thing. He talked about engineering and prototyping. Each time he made a new point, he would snap his finger and it would do a nearly perfect jump cut to a new background. It might be a visual of him working on cars or a video of him at the local makerspace.

When it was finished, he came alive during this question-and-answer process. Ricardo found his voice that year. He embraced his love of technology and helped program our Linux computers. He got into circuitry and magnetism during our roller coaster projects. He embraced blogging and even podcasting, despite his nervousness in speaking in front of a group.

Nearly a decade later, Ricardo is an engineer. Many of the technology skills he learned are now obsolete. But there are certain skills that have become essential for him in an every-changing world: creativity, collaboration, communication, iterative thinking, empathy, and resilience.

DEVELOPING HUMAN SKILLS IN AN A.I. WORLD

In the first chapter, I mentioned the need for students to develop human skills in a world of A.I. One of the best ways for students to develop these skills is through authentic project-based learning. PBL is a teaching method that focuses on active, experiential learning through the completion of real-world projects. Students tackle an authentic problem, and they work collaboratively to design, create, and present their solution.[84]

The goal of project-based learning is to engage students in deeper learning experiences that are relevant to their lives and interests. PBL centers the learning on human skills that the A.I. can't do. Here students develop critical social-emotional learning skills. It's an idea Mike Kaechele and Matinga Ragatz explored in-depth in *Pulse of PBL*.[85] Instead of teaching individual SEL lessons in a traditional way, students develop key SEL competencies through projects. In other words, they develop these skills by doing projects not merely learning about the skills through a traditional lesson plan.

EVERY STUDENT DESERVES ACCESS TO PROJECT-BASED LEARNING

Project-based learning can help facilitate SEL skills by creating the context for students to engage in social-emotional learning. At the same time, when students also engage in this hands-on social-emotional learning, they develop the very skills that help them create better projects. This leads to a reciprocal relationship, where PBL leads to SEL and SEL improves student performance in PBL tasks.

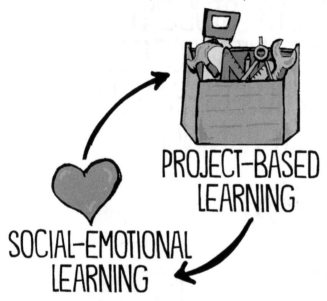

I realize the term SEL has become politically charged lately.[86] Certain opponents view it as a form of brainwashing. However, when we simply look at the competencies as defined by CASEL,[87] SEL is something that people from across the political spectrum can all agree on. In other words, SEL is not a liberal or conservative idea. It's a universal idea. At its core, SEL is about helping students develop the critical skills they'll need to navigate a complex world.

Project-based learning provides the perfect context for students to engage in social-emotional learning and SEL provides a chance for students to learn about the key skills that will allow students to thrive in collaborative projects.

Mike Kaechele and Matinga Ragatz do a phenomenal job taking a deeper dive into the overlap of SEL and PBL. I highly recommend checking out their book (also published by Blend Education). However, I'd like to focus more specifically on why this matters in an age of A.I.

In an age of machine learning, self-awareness is more vital than ever. Our students will need to wrestle with hard questions regarding what it means to be human in an era dominated by smart machines.

Projects provide an excellent context for the SEL competency of responsible decision-making. Our students will need to think above the algorithms. They'll need to ask hard ethical questions about the ways we engage in machine learning an A.I. Responsible decision-making includes the big ethical questions students will need to ask about how we design and implement our A.I. systems.

A.I. systems are not infallible. They are only as good as the data they are trained on and the algorithms that are used to process that data. Humans play a crucial role in identifying and correcting errors and biases in A.I. systems, ensuring that they are used ethically and responsibly.

Let's consider the competency of social awareness. A.I. systems will impact our society in profound ways with both negative and positive consequences that we can't predict. Our students will need to be aware of how these changes are occurring in real-time. As A.I. systems become more integrated into our lives and society, it is essential that our students have a deep understanding of the social and ethical implications of their use.

PBL BY DESIGN

Project-based learning focuses on active, experiential learning through the completion of real-world projects. Students are given a problem or challenge to solve, and they work collaboratively to design, create, and present their solution. When coupled with design thinking, students develop the critical human skills that they will need as they navigate a changing world.

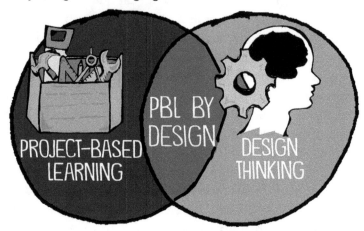

Here, students embrace a maker mindset. They define themselves as inventors and creators. They learn to take creative risks. They experiment and engage in iterative thinking. When this happens, they embrace a growth mindset and grow resilient. They become problem solvers and systems thinkers. They use creative constraint to find original uses for materials. Here, they discover it's okay to be different. Often students embrace curiosity and wonder. They become explorers seeking out new information and thinking critically. They grow more empathetic as they design meaningful products that they launch to the world.

On an academic level, students are more engaged and the information sticks.[88] There's often an increase in student achievement. Meanwhile, they learn key skills like project management, collaboration, and communication. True, these projects will prepare students for the creative economy. But more importantly, they empower students for a creative life.

Think of it this way. PBL is the pedagogical framework. Design thinking is the creative framework. When you combine design thinking and project-based learning, students engage in authentic projects that lead to deeper learning and ultimately help students develop the human skills they'll need in an unpredictable world of A.I.

HOW WOULD YOU USE A.I. IN PBL?

So, as we think about student projects, we will likely anchor student work on human skills like collaboration, creativity, empathy, and divergent thinking. However, we want to avoid the Techno Futurism trap of outsourcing too much of the thinking to the A.I. In other words, students will still come up with questions, create content, generate ideas, sketch out plans, and give feedback even if it's something that an A.I. could do. At the same time, we can leverage the power of A.I. in projects. Here's a sample of ideas:

- **Conceptual development:** Early in the project stage, students can ask questions to define vocabulary and develop a deeper conceptual understanding of the content. This can help increase each student's background knowledge.
- **Generating additional questions:** Toward the beginning of a project, a student might start with a list of research questions they have.. If they're asking interview questions, they could ask the A.I. to refine their questions to be more open-ended or convey more critical thinking. Notice how they're not outsourcing the inquiry, but they are using A.I. as a tool.
- **Clarifying misconceptions during research:** Sometimes students struggle to understand key concepts. A question-and-answer session with an A.I. chatbot can be a powerful way to build that deeper conceptual understanding.
- **Restating research in simpler terms:** If students are doing text-based research, they might see a website with great research. They've looked at the reliability of the source and explored

the bias. Unfortunately, the source contains technical language and dense grammatical structures. Students then use A.I. to simplify the language.

- **Navigating ideas:** After students have engaged in a deep dive brainstorm, they can go to A.I. and ask for additional ideas. Students can then analyze these ideas and incorporate them into their design.
- **Generating project plans:** After they have navigated ideas, students can use A.I. as a starting place for a project plan with dates and deadlines. They can then modify this based on their skill level, group dynamics, etc. We'll explore this more in-depth later in this chapter as we analyze what it looks like to use A.I. for project management.
- **Prototyping:** If students are writing code, they might start with A.I. and then modify the code to make it better. The A.I. might create that initial "vanilla" that students modify with their own unique spin.
- **Feedback:** As students work through the PBL process, A.I. chatbots can provide vital feedback that they use to modify their designs.
- **Coming up with group roles:** Students can use A.I. as a starting place for group roles and then modify them to fit the group. The group can then use A.I. to create group contracts with norms, roles, and consequences.

We need to be cognizant of the policies and permissions in using A.I. with students. But I think it's important that we ask, "How will students someday use A.I. in different industries and how can we anticipate it as we design PBL units?" One of those key areas within nearly every industry is project management. Let's take a look at how we might use A.I. within that process.

THE FOUR COMPONENTS
PROJECT MANAGEMENT

#1
SET GOALS AND CHART PROGRESS

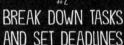

#2
BREAK DOWN TASKS AND SET DEADLINES

NOTE THAT EACH OF THESE PHASES CAN OFTEN WORK IN TANDEM RATHER THAN SEQUENTIALLY.

#3
CHOOSE AND IMPLEMENT SPECIFIC STRATEGIES

#4
MONITOR, ADJUST AND PROBLEM-SOLVE

USING A.I. AS A PROJECT MANAGEMENT TOOL

If you do a quick search online, you'll see tons of different project management models, apps, and programs. While the programs vary, the important thing is that students are engaged in the project management process. Here are four key components to project management. I'd like to share a few ways we can use A.I. to help with each aspect of this project management process.

1. SET GOALS AND CHART PROGRESS

Project management begins with goal setting. Students need to have a clear sense of where they are going and what it will look like when they are finished. Here's where A.I. can be helpful. Students might take the project instructions or the project rubric and create their own goals. They can then use a chatbot to generate a set of project goals and see if they want to add some of the goals that the chatbot creates as well. These goals will drive the next component of breaking down the tasks.

2. BREAK DOWN TASKS AND SET DEADLINES

After students create goals, they can then break the project down into tasks and subtasks with clear setting deadlines. When students set realistic deadlines, they can turn a project from an idea into a reality.

In this phase, students need to think realistically about what is needed in terms of time, resources, and concrete actions. Students develop a plan of action and select their tools and materials. If it's a collaborative project, students often divide up roles and responsibilities.

Chatbots can help students refine their project ideas by providing guidance on narrowing down the scope, identifying specific objectives, and setting achievable milestones. Students might ask the chatbot to provide a project plan by dividing the project into smaller tasks, assigning responsibilities to team members, and establishing a timeline for completion. Students can then modify the initial plan (tasks, subtasks, and deadlines) to fit their own context.

Other times, students might use a chatbot to provide feedback on the plan they've created. Chatbots can help students identify potential challenges and risks associated with their project goals and suggest strategies to mitigate them. Students might ask a question like, "Is this a realistic timeline? What might we need to adjust?"

3. CHOOSE AND IMPLEMENT STRATEGIES

Once they have a clear plan, students begin to choose and implement their specific strategies. They can select the resources and materials while also deciding on the processes that will work best for them. So, when doing research, they might use notecards or a spreadsheet. When managing their project, they might keep their tasks on a shared document or on a shared calendar.

Here's where a chatbot can be a game-changer with students who need a checklist to improve their focus. Students can take their assigned tasks and ask for a detailed checklist with time deadlines based on the class period.

4. MONITOR, ADJUST, AND PROBLEM-SOLVE

While tasks and deadlines are vital to project management, things will not always work according to plan. Students can have the best-developed plans in the world, but life will happen. The internet goes down for a day. A group member gets sick for two days. You have a fire drill and then an unplanned assembly. A few students hit a creative block and suddenly feel stuck.

In these moments, students will need to solve problems and deal with issues as they arise. Things will break. Plans will change. This is the frustrating side of student-centered learning. It's messier than a tidy worksheet. And yet, when students are able to tackle these challenges, they grow into problem-solvers and critical thinkers. They can monitor their progress and adjust their approach as they go.

In this phase, students will also monitor and perhaps even re-examine their original goals. Students can use a chatbot to reflect on their performance, assess the achievement of their goals, and identify areas for improvement or further exploration. So, they might put in a prompt asking for a revised set of goals. They might ask the chatbot to change their timeline or offer suggestions for how to speed things up.

USE A.I. WISELY

While chatbots can provide valuable support, it's essential for students to engage in critical thinking, collaborate with their peers, and consult with their teachers to ensure the success of their PBL experience. We don't want to turn the project management process over to an A.I. entirely. Instead, we should integrate chatbots into PBL in a way that is human-driven.

Project-based learning is more relevant than ever because it equips students with human skills that machines cannot replace. At the same time, it's an opportunity to use A.I. in a way that is authentic, ethical, and creative.

CHAPTER 9

REDEFINING
ASSESSMENT PRACTICES
IN A WORLD OF A.I.

"He's not supposed to have that," a professor whispers, as he points to a small plastic bottle.

"What is it?" I ask.

"It's an energy shot. Like the Five Hour Energy drinks you have in the United States," he whispers back.

I'm standing here in China, watching the students recite back an answer in a choral response. The teacher enthusiastically explains a grammatical concept in English while pointing to her interactive whiteboard. On another flatscreen reads a leaderboard with a series of scores.

"What is that?" I ask the professor.

"Those are the student engagement scores," he tells me.

I watch the students sitting up straight, answering questions, and scribbling notes. On the surface, there's nearly 100% engagement. I see no cell phones, no passing notes, no giggling, and no off-task whispering. Even when they move to a think-pair-share activity, nearly every student participates.

The scores update every few minutes, but the teacher doesn't seem to record anything.

"Wait, who's giving the students their engagement score?" I ask.

He points to the cameras but says nothing. All at once, it makes sense. The cameras aren't there to record the lesson for students who are home sick. These are facial recognition cameras that scan each student every thirty seconds. The boy with the energy shot? He's trying to stay focused after a late-night studying. A dip in engagement might not be a big deal. But the score is part of the larger system that might eventually determine what university each student will someday attend.

Fast forward six years. The technology has grown more complex. New facial recognition software can categorize student actions with the hopes of finding students who are "at risk" of misbehaving. In other words, it promises to catch misbehavior before it occurs.[89] [90]

This vision for integrating A.I. in assessment focuses on surveillance, scoring, and ranking. I bristle at the dystopian undertones of this approach but it's a reminder that our values drive our assessment processes.

This is just one of many ways we might see schools use A.I. for assessment purposes. Let's consider the following ways machine learning might be used in student assessment. For each one, rank from 1-5 whether you believe a school should use this type of A.I. A score of a 1 would be a *no way we should do this* and a 5 would be an *absolutely we should do this.*

_____ **Plagiarism Detector:** A.I. can be used to detect plagiarism in student work by comparing it to a large database of existing work. In theory, this can help to ensure academic integrity and discourage cheating.

_____ **Predictive Analytics:** The A.I. analyzes student performance data to identify trends and predict future performance. Teachers can then intervene early when a student is struggling and provide targeted support. Why wait for a kid to struggle if you know they're going to struggle? Intervene before they need intervention. The A.I. explores patterns of past students and identify a struggling student early so we don't have to take a reactive approach to assessment.

_____ **Automated Grading:** A.I. can be used to automate the grading of assignments and exams, reducing the workload for teachers and providing faster feedback to students. A.I. can also be used to grade essays. This is done through natural language processing (NLP) algorithms that analyze the text for things like grammar, sentence structure, and coherence.

_____ **Behavioral Analysis**: A.I. can be used to analyze student behavior and engagement in the classroom. For example, A.I. can track eye movements, facial expressions, and body language to assess engagement and understanding.

_____ **Adaptive Learning:** A.I. can be used to develop personalized learning paths for students based on their individual strengths and weaknesses. Adaptive learning systems use A.I. algorithms to adjust the difficulty of questions based on a student's performance, providing a more customized learning experience.

_____ **Audio Recognition:** A.I. can be used to analyze student responses during class discussions and provide feedback on their communication skills. Students can then get an overall score on voice, diction, clarity, and tone. A.I. can also listen to choirs to provide feedback to improve their performances. Similarly, A.I. can listen to bands and individual musicians to determine how well students are playing individual notes.

If you're like me, some of these ideas elicit a strong emotional reaction. It goes beyond being merely an ineffective strategy. Some of these uses of A.I. might cause deep harm to children (such as the predictive analysis for student misbehavior). Others feel like time-saving assessments that could free up teachers to spend more time on things like student conferencing.

However, this is precisely why we need to think about the bigger "why" of assessment before asking how we might incorporate A.I. into assessment practices.

BEFORE ASKING,
"HOW CAN WE USE
AI IN ASSESSMENT?"
WE MIGHT WANT TO ASK,
"WHAT IS THE PURPOSE
OF ASSESSMENT?"

WHAT DO WE MEAN BY ASSESSMENT?

When I teach the assessment design course, I've noticed that pre-service teachers feel strong emotions about assessment. Do we give extra credit? If so, are we valuing accuracy or effort? Do we take points off for late work? If so, is this about measuring the mastery of learning or teaching students how to stick to deadlines and work hard? Should we grade for effort or grade based upon a set of criteria? Do we give group grades on projects or is that unfair to individuals who did all the work? Should we use weighted categories? Should students get the opportunity to resubmit work or retake tests? If so, does that help them gain perseverance or lead to laziness?

I have watched teachers engage in heated debates over these issues. These assessment practices are rooted in our values about fairness and justice. They connect to what we believe about teaching and learning. Tell me to try a new discussion protocol with small groups? I'm down for that. Tell me to eliminate zeroes from the grade book? I've got strong feelings about it.

As we think about the role of A.I. and assessment, we need to recognize that machine learning will not occur in a vacuum. Values, beliefs, and policies will shape the way engineers design and educators implement these A.I. systems. As a teacher, leader, or coach, it can help to look at any A.I. assessment tool and ask, "What are the values driving this design?"

Many of the A.I. assessment tools I've explored are driven by a behaviorist perspective of learning. These often place an emphasis on surveillance and accountability. Think plagiarism detectors or facial recognition systems used to gauge student engagement. However, others are quasi-behaviorist with elements of gamification, including badges, points, levels, and leaderboards. Still others use generative A.I. like a personal assistant who guides students in personal reflection. Some A.I. assessment tools treat knowledge as something obtained, retained, and explained rather than internally constructed. But others are more dynamic and responsive, recognizing the value of a student's schema in learning. Some assessment tools are more diagnostic, others more descriptive (providing an "extra set of eyes" to guide reflection), and others evaluative.

My fear is that we will see A.I. assessment tools chosen largely by convenience and cost rather than pedagogical soundness or core values. I worry that we will see tools gain popularity due to clever marketing. As districts purchase these tools in a top-down fashion, some educational leaders will push for compliance in the name of using common assessments. Instead of providing a tool and trusting teachers to decide when and how to use it, we could end up with policies that outsource most of the assessment processes to a machine. Meanwhile, these systems might conflict with a teacher's core beliefs.

Note that this isn't new. We've seen teachers lose professional autonomy when districts purchase multiple choice assessment systems for benchmark tests. But this has the potential to be more pervasive because of the convenience and low costs of these tools. I'm not opposed to using A.I. for assessment. I've seen how well certain generative A.I. can function in providing quality feedback. But I am concerned with the notion of outsourcing the assessment process to a machine and thus stripping educators of their agency in assessment.

I've seen too many policies promising to "save time" and "make your jobs easier" that actually cause more stress and reduce professional agency and autonomy (consider the pervasive use of scripted curriculum). On the other hand, if educators are empowered to use A.I. tools wisely, we will end up with a more human-driven approach moving forward.

At a basic level, most of us can agree that assessment exists for a few reasons:

- **Assessment helps teachers know how individual students are doing.** Did this student master the learning target? Does this student understand the concepts? Has this student mastered the skills? Is this student engaged in the learning? Does the student need additional supports or scaffolds? These questions help us identify which students need enrichment and which need intervention.
- **Assessment helps teachers know how the larger class is doing.** What are the overall trends that you notice? What are students understanding and failing to understand? Do we need to make any modifications to our unit plans? These questions help teachers with the larger lesson planning cycle of planning, implementing, and assessing.
- **Assessment helps students know their mastery level.** Students should be able to articulate what they know, what they don't know, and where they will go next. Assessment might also help increase student motivation or self-efficacy. It might be less evaluative and be more descriptive.

WHAT DOES THIS LOOK LIKE?

The following are three scenarios where a teacher might use A.I. in their assessment practices. While these are fictionalized accounts, the tools and processes are real based on a composite of interviews I've done with multiple teachers. Notice that the teachers are using A.I. tools but doing so in a way that's driven by the context of their classroom, the pedagogy of the content area, and a human-centered assessment approach.

3ᴿᴰ GRADE LANGUAGE ARTS CLASS

DeAndre is teaching his students how to write informational texts. The driving standard asks students to write informative/explanatory texts to examine a topic and convey ideas and information clearly. He has also chosen a connecting standard that asks students to develop and strengthen writing as needed by revising and editing. Finally, he's asking students to produce clear and coherent writing in which the development, organization, and style are appropriate to task, purpose, and audience.

Students type up their initial drafts on a shared Google Document and now he wants to give formative feedback. For this, he's focusing on organization, style, and ideas (conveying ideas and information clearly). Instead of creating a rubric from scratch, he uses ChatGPT to create a rubric.

The initial rubric looks like this:

Organization

4 - The writing has a clear introduction, body, and conclusion with well-organized paragraphs that flow smoothly.

3 - The writing has an introduction, body, and conclusion, but the organization could be improved with more transitions and better paragraph structure.

2 - The writing has an introduction, body, and conclusion, but the organization is confusing and difficult to follow.

1 - The writing lacks clear organization and does not have a proper introduction, body, or conclusion.

Style

4 - The writing demonstrates a consistent and appropriate tone throughout, using varied and descriptive language that engages the reader.

3 - The writing has an appropriate tone and uses some descriptive language, but could benefit from more variety and depth.

2 - The writing has a somewhat inappropriate tone and limited use of descriptive language, making it less engaging to the reader.

1 - The writing has an inappropriate tone and uses minimal descriptive language, resulting in a dull and uninteresting piece.

Ideas
4 - The writing demonstrates a clear understanding of the prompt, showing creativity and originality in its ideas and perspectives.
3 - The writing demonstrates an understanding of the prompt, with some creative and original ideas, but could benefit from more depth and detail.
2 - The writing partially addresses the prompt, but lacks creativity and originality, resulting in a predictable and uninspired piece.
1 - The writing does not address the prompt and lacks any creativity or originality, resulting in an incomplete and uninteresting piece.

Overall Score: 12-10: Excellent 9-7: Good 6-4: Fair 3-1: Poor

DeAndre wants to keep the feedback formative while using a standards-based approach. He knows, for example, that a composite score isn't accurate. Instead, he'd rather students know how they did in each category. He also wants it to be in student-friendly language. So, he ends up with the following:

	Beginning	Getting Closer	Meets	Exceeds
Organization	The writing has some parts, but they are not in order or easy to follow.	The writing has all the parts, but they need better transitions to connect them together.	The writing has all the parts in order and it is easy to understand.	The writing has all the parts in order and it flows smoothly with great transitions.
Style	The writing sounds wrong and it is boring to read.	The writing needs more describing words to make it more interesting.	The writing has good describing words and it is fun to read.	The writing has amazing describing words that make it very interesting and fun to read.

Ideas	The writing does not answer the question and it is not interesting.	The writing answers the question, but it is not creative or interesting.	The writing answers the question and has some creative and interesting ideas.	The writing answers the question with very creative and interesting ideas that are well-developed.

This is a solid start, but DeAndre doesn't like the "creative or interesting" parts. Instead, he revises the rubric to focus on using facts to back up ideas and staying on-topic. He reworks the rubric until he has something that he likes. Typically, it takes him two hours to make a rubric. This time, it takes about 25 minutes. Notice that the A.I. is merely a tool. DeAndre remains the content and pedagogical expert.

As he grades the student work, DeAndre uses a chatbot to help come up with a list of 4 glows (positive aspects) and 1 grow (area to improve). He blends his ideas with those of the chatbot. He next uses an A.I. scheduler look at his weekly calendar and set up 14 student conferences (roughly 3 per day) so he can do writing conferences with each student every other week.

DeAndre uses A.I. to save time and free him up to do more of the relational aspects of the assessment process. For him, A.I. is like a time-saving teacher's assistant which can free him the tedium of testing so he can focus on what matters most.

ALGEBRA II CLASS

Samira uses a set of 5 different word problems to assess whether students understand polynomial factorization. Each student receives a different randomized quiz generator with the same five problems. Students use the camera app on their web cams to take pictures of their work and then type in the answers. Once submitted, the A.I. automatically grades their work. The term "grade" here is misleading. Every student gets credit for completing this quiz and reflecting on what they did right, what they did wrong, and what they'll do next.

At this moment, Samira has a snapshot of the entire class. She knows how many of the students successfully completed the quiz (demonstrating computational fluency) and how each student did on each problem. But she still eyeballs each test to see what kinds of mistakes students are making. For this, she uses a quick rubric of each component of factoring polynomials. She feels that the process takes longer than it should.

Eventually, she adopts an A.I. program that provides data on the common mistakes students are making and recommendations for what she needs to reteach. She uses the individual data to craft targeted interventions that she generates using an A.I. chatbot. On a student level, she encourages the use of programs a phone-based app for instant feedback and the use of chatbots to clarify misunderstandings.

For Samira, the A.I. goes beyond a time-saving device. What she really wants is a diagnostic tool that can give students feedback and offer tutorials to help them figure out what to do next. She wants to build their self-efficacy in Algebra II and she worries that a slow pace of teacher feedback isn't giving students the corrective help they need. She looks forward to the day when students get real-time feedback during class so that she can focus on the dynamic, conversational forms of feedback she can engage in while she walks around and helps each small group.

Samira is excited about the newer possibilities of A.I. in math assessment because of the speed of the feedback and the ability to find trends and patterns in student mistakes in a way that she simply can't pick up on every time.

PE CLASS

Ash is a PE teacher who also coaches softball and track. She uses an A.I. program to help students set up goals in her weightlifting and personal fitness classes. Each student gets a personalized fitness workout and then tracks it in their PE notebooks. She is impressed by the gamification elements that help students progress from easily attainable goals to bigger goals.

Ash also uses a video feedback program that analyzes each softball player's swing. Together, athletes meet in pairs to discuss their metrics and examine key recommendations from the A.I. on what changes need to be made in their swings. Ash uses advanced data metrics to decide the team's game line-up and decide on key softball decisions. However, she is not comfortable with the predictive analytics that forecast which players will grow and improve over the season. So, she's both excited about the use of A.I. in assessment but also skeptical about anything that veers into predictive analytics. You can't predict something like mental toughness.

Notice how each of these teachers are using A.I. in a different way for assessment. For some, it's about improving teacher productivity. For others, the key is speed of the feedback. For others, it's about providing feedback that teachers might miss due to human error. Notice, too, how the content area impacts the process as well. In one area it might be more performance-based while another one is about clarifying concepts or finding mistakes in a process. But in each case, teachers are the assessment experts who decide when and how to integrate A.I. into the process.

We can't predict how A.I. will change the assessment process but there are a few likely trends that will change the way we assess our students. Check out the sketchnote on the following page.

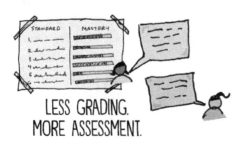

LESS GRADING.
MORE ASSESSMENT.

FASTER FEEDBACK

HOW MIGHT A.I. CHANGE ASSESSMENT PRACTICES?

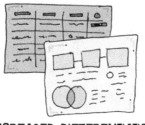

INCREASED DIFFERENTIATION
IN ASSESSMENTS

MORE PRECISION
IN FEEDBACK

PREDICTIVE ANALYTICS

EMPOWERING STUDENTS
TO OWN THE ASSESSMENT
PROCESS

AUTO-GRADING
EXPANDING TO AUDIO
AND VIDEO

WHAT ABOUT STUDENT OWNERSHIP?

Most of this chapter has been about assessment through the lens of a teacher. However, students might also use A.I. to assess their progress and plan their next moves. This needs to be developmentally appropriate and follow clear policy guidelines. However, here is what it might look like:

Goal-Setting: Students can use A.I. to get personalized recommendations for areas to improve. They can take ownership of the learning process by evaluating their strengths and weaknesses and coming up with next steps.

Resource Recommendations: Students can use A.I. as a curation device to help find the scaffolds, tutorials, and resources they need when learning a concept. Whether it's a set of tutorials in an applied math exploration or a recommendation of sites to visit in a PBL, A.I. has the potential for students to move from "What do I need to know?" to "Where can I find this?"

Performance Feedback and Reflection: The combination of video and A.I. can provide quality feedback on physical performances. Imagine having A.I. listen to a musical practice and give targeted feedback. Students can also ask the A.I. for specific feedback.

Learning Portfolios: We tend to think of digital portfolios as a personal endeavor – which it is. But they are also inherently social. Students are sharing their work with a larger audience. A.I. can be used to help students create and maintain digital portfolios, which can showcase their achievements and growth over time. A student might select three artifacts and then choose two more from a recommendation algorithm.

Time Management: A.I. can be used to help students manage their time more effectively, by providing personalized reminders and recommendations for how to prioritize their tasks. If a student is working on a project and finding social media distracting, they might use A.I. to create a system to stay focused. However, there's also a time for ignoring metrics and embracing human inefficiency. Daydreaming, going for walks, taking brain breaks – these all lead to better problem-solving and improved creativity.

Facilitating Reflection: Assessment isn't always purely evaluative. Sometimes it's more descriptive in nature. Students can work with chatbots to facilitate reflection in a way that allows for follow up questions. Here, the A.I. works in a role-playing approach to help students reflect on their mastery of the standards.

Personalized Feedback: Students can submit an example and get immediate feedback. It could be diagnostic feedback to help determine mistakes. Or it could be an open-ended set of pros and cons.

REMEMBER THE HUMAN ELEMENT

I showed my son how well ChatGPT does in analyzing writing and giving targeted feedback. I explained that it could do feedback almost instantaneously in a way that I, as a teacher, cannot. I gave an example of one of my blog posts. It was a personal narrative about the lessons our greyhound taught me.

His response?

"That's horrible feedback."

"What do you mean? It's practical and actionable. It includes more positive than negative feedback. Everything about it is true."

My son said, "If a teacher did that it would be heartless. If someone writes about their pet who just died, the only response is 'I'm so sorry. Want to talk about it?' That's it. You can give feedback later."

He went on to say "Feedback is fine. I know that we need it and all, but my favorite English teachers give feedback in a way that makes me feel known. The feedback makes me want to write. It's critical, yeah, but it's critical in a way where I think, 'My teacher gets me.' Does that make sense?"

It does make sense. What he's alluding to is that feedback isn't mechanical. It's relational. It's dynamic. It's contextual. It's even, at times, empathetic. While there's immense potential in A.I. as a feedback tool, it shouldn't replace the relational aspect of assessment.

At the most human level, assessment is a conversation. Sometimes it's an internal dialogue we do in isolation. Sometimes it's a conversation with trusted peers. Often, it's a conversation between a student and a teacher. These conversations might be about word choice or style or argumentation. But they might also be about hopes and dreams and grief and loss. I never want to lose those conversations.

A.I. can function as a form of peer feedback. The algorithm can generate targeted feedback on voice and style and word choice. It can help me tighten up my writing ~~to get rid of unnecessary words that I don't need to use~~. But it can't tell me what it's like for a person to read it. For that, I need a human on the other end who can say, "John that piece moved me."

That's the kind of feedback that makes me want to write more.

My hope is that A.I. can free teachers up to focus on the human aspects of assessment. Many of my current students (preservice teachers at the elementary level) spend hours testing students on reading fluency. In the upcoming years, we will likely have A.I. that can listen to students do fluency practice and catch the mistakes to provide a fluency score and diagnose areas where they might be struggling in phonics, blending, and phonemic awareness. This would free teachers up to do one-on-one conferencing. My hope is that A.I. will free teachers up to give the kind of feedback that only a human can give.

CHAPTER 10
REDEFINING PERSONALIZED LEARNING IN A WORLD OF A.I.

Eight students stood in line whispering to one another. A few of them had peeked into the windows to see what was new. One girl had a tiny notebook with a list. Most of the students had pulled out their phones to check key information.

There was a buzz in the air that settled into an intense, quiet excitement. But this wasn't a concert or a line to buy smart phones or the front gate of a sporting event. This was our first library day of the school year.

A boy walked up to me and asked, "What are you going to get?"

"I already have a book I'm reading," I answered.

He shook his head. "Nah, Spencer, you have to check out something. Everyone leaves with at least two books but no more than five."

"Is that a rule?" I asked.

He laughed. A rule? It was like making a rule that you must eat an ice cream sundae or binge-watch your favorite show. No, it wasn't a rule. It was a gift.

Right then, the librarian opened the door and waved her hands in the air as if she were awkwardly doing the classic "raise the roof" dance move. The students streamed in . . . loudly. They scurried from display to display, reading the back covers, and debating books. Our librarian seemed to embrace the noise as she called out specific books.

"Carlos! You'll love this one," she yelled from across the library. Some of the students had been checking out books all summer but she had built up "release dates" for the first week of school. She knew that the library, like a great novel, was all about suspense. Yes, it should be accessible. True, it should be easy to navigate. But it should also build up anticipation.

The cynical side of me had initially scoffed at middle school students getting this excited about books. There is a cultural perception that reading is inherently uncool. But any cynicism I felt began to melt as I watched the sincerity of my students. They were pulling out their phones and reading the QR codes to get book reviews. They debated the merits of various series and, on occasion, mocked other students for their choices in novels (something I would address in our first whole class meeting). The library was a candy store for the mind.

At one point, the librarian called students to an open space and reminded them of some strategies for finding the right book. She talked about reading sample pages, checking out the synopsis on the back of the book, reading the 3-Star Amazon Reviews (which often provides the most measured review of the pros and cons of a work) and even looking at the book covers to see who they were marketing it toward. Was she actually asking us to judge a book by its cover?

This library experience defied the stereotypes of the stodgy, quiet library. But I've found that the silent library stereotype is misguided. Librarians are finding innovative ways to spark student excitement about reading – our school was no exception.

Our school librarian was a leader of an empowered community. She was an expert in reading, curation, media literacy, and library science. But she never presented herself as the sole expert in reading. Instead, she built relationships with students and worked with them to find texts that would connect with their interests. As a true curator, she read a broad variety of books and constantly explored new authors and genres with the hopes of helping students fall in love with reading. She was also a master architect who designed systems that would empower students. She worked with teams of students to do book talks and book preview videos.

In other words, she helped design the ecosystem of reading that would allow me, as the teacher, to build a classroom culture of empowered readers. This moment was a reminder of the power of personalized learning. But I contrast this to a different experience I had with teaching reading.

THE LIBRARY
FELT LIKE A TRIP TO THE
CANDY STORE

WHAT DO WE MEAN BY PERSONALIZED LEARNING?

"Here's the booklet. It tells you exactly what to do to help students get into the reading intervention software. Everything should stay inside the program. It's cloud-based but it's been downloaded, meaning students really can't go onto the internet, even if they tried," the district representative explained.

"What do I do?" I asked.

"Walk around. Monitor. If they have any questions, they'll raise their hands," he explains.

"But what about the small group discussions?" I ask.

"No need for that. The whole program is personalized. There are no discussions," he answers.

"No Lit circles?" I ask.

"No, it's fully individualized. This is state-of-the-art adaptive learning. That means they'll get vocabulary practice and reading intervention work that targets their key deficiencies. You don't have to do any assessment. I mean, yes, once a week, you'll read the printout to them and talk about their goals. But it's driven by the adaptive learning software. You'll get data on how well they master every standard. As they move up to higher reading levels, they'll get badges."

"And what do I do?" I asked.

"Just monitor them," he says. "It's honestly the easiest class you'll ever teach. This is the future of reading intervention. Personalized learning is finally a reality, John."

As I implemented the program, I couldn't help but feel that "personalized" was the wrong word. If anything, it felt impersonal. Students sat at computers doing digital worksheets meant to teach everything from phonics and blending to reading comprehension. They wore headphones as I walked between the rows and kept students on track. This was the first glimpse of adaptive learning fueled by A.I. A series of cryptic algorithms set the tone and pace of the learning. I simply watched.

Three weeks later, I approached my principal with a new idea. After nearly a semester of this adaptive learning program (with a previous teacher and now myself), students weren't reaching their reading goals. They were bored and frustrated. We assumed that the program simply needing more data and some targeted adjustments. But what if we had it all wrong? What if our whole premise of personalized learning was built on the wrong foundation?

I pitched a different idea. We would head out to the library and choose books. Students would read silently each day and build up reading endurance.[91] We would use recommendations from algorithms but also lean heavily on our amazing librarian. We would form literary circles and do shared read alouds. But we would also log onto the adaptive learning program to do five to ten minutes of prescriptive phonics, blending, and morphology work. After all, you can't fall in love with reading when you can't actually decode. We wouldn't avoid A.I., but we wouldn't let the machines drive the learning. Instead, our focus would remain on the human connection and then amplify it with the A.I. system.

Four weeks later, we compared this new approach to the previous adaptive learning program. It turned out our students had higher reading scores than the district average for those in reading intervention. By focusing on motivation and building up reading endurance, students improved on their overall scores. While other students did well on the first few problems and then struggled later in the test, my students remained consistent and thus outperformed their peers in the long run.

I would never claim that adaptive learning programs don't work. Emerging research suggests that their implementation can lead to gains in reading achievement scores.[92] Nor would I claim that my experience is normative. But it was a reminder that personalized learning must begin with the person rather than the machine.

ADAPTIVE LEARNING IS MACHINE-DRIVEN

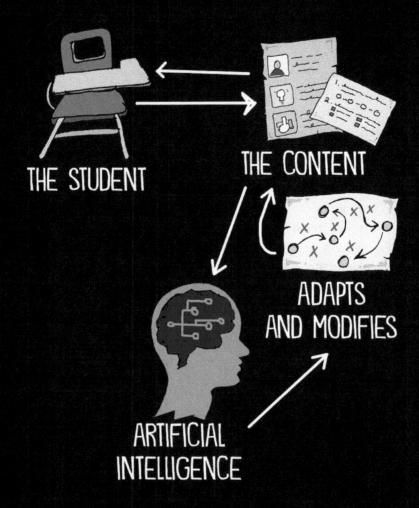

THE STUDENT

THE CONTENT

ADAPTS AND MODIFIES

ARTIFICIAL INTELLIGENCE

PERSONALIZED LEARNING IS HUMAN-DRIVEN. THE AI IS MERELY A TOOL.

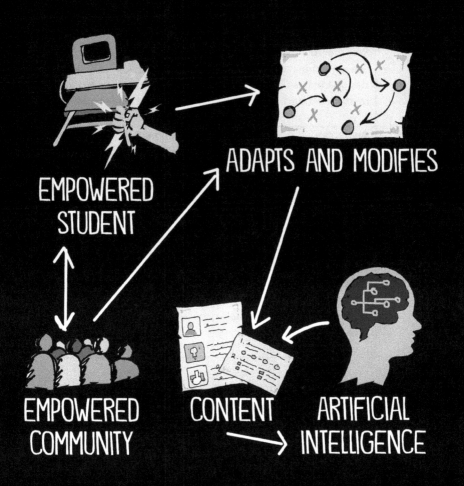

EMPOWERED STUDENT

ADAPTS AND MODIFIES

EMPOWERED COMMUNITY

CONTENT

ARTIFICIAL INTELLIGENCE

PERSONALIZED LEARNING OR ADAPTIVE LEARNING?

The line between personalized learning and adaptive learning is blurry. In some contexts, people use these terms interchangeably. But for this book, I make the distinction that personalized learning is human-centered and adaptive learning is machine-centered. I make the following distinctions between the two:

	Personalized Learning	Adaptive Learning
Structure	**Human-Driven** Personalized learning might use algorithms to inform the design but it is ultimately human-centered.	**Algorithm-Driven** Students progress through pre-set curriculum and the A.I. adapts the levels to the skill level and interests of students.
Learning Tasks	**Authentic** Students engage in authentic problem-solving. There are opportunities to do creative work.	**Programmed** Students don't have as many opportunities to connect to the world or to solve authentic problems. Often, they work on targeted standards using digital worksheets.
Grouping	**Collaborative** Personalized learning requires interdependent student work. Even when students work on individual projects, they engage in peer feedback.	**Individualized** Students work alone at a computer. The work is at their level and follows their pace.

Assessment	**Varied** Students engage in self-reflections, peer feedback, and teacher assessments. They might even use A.I. but it's simply one of many options.	**Singular** Students might engage in a self-reflection as an assignment, but the A.I. is at the heart of the assessment process. It's fast and efficient. Students get immediate feedback and the algorithm uses the assessment data to adjust the next learning task.
Process	**Messy** While personalized learning still leans into structures and scaffolds, the process is often messy.	**Efficient** Adaptive learning tends to move efficiently with specific feedback and adjustments happening in the moment.
Role of the Learner	**Empowers the Learner:** Genuine personalized learning focuses on learner agency. There's a sense of freedom.	**Engages the Learner:** Adaptive learning is less about agency and more about providing targeted instruction. Students might get choices but they have no real voice in the process.
Role of the Teacher	**Active Facilitator:** The teacher plays the role of instructional designer and often takes a step back as the "guide on the side" giving individual feedback or pulling small groups. But the teacher also engages in direct instruction and leads whole class activities.	**Passive Manager:** The teacher might still do some tutoring or pull-outs by having the whole class use the adaptive learning program while they act as an active facilitator. But within most adaptive learning programs, the teacher is the manager of the system. Teachers review the data and make sure students are on task.

There's nothing inherently wrong with adaptive learning programs. In Chapter 18, we'll explore how these programs can help in a world language course. In terms of reading intervention, adaptive learning programs work well for targeted skill practice. But we need to be cognizant of the false promise that A.I. will provide personalized learning for all learning tasks.

Generative A.I. promises to take adaptive learning to the next level. This newer generation will not only provide leveled work, but it will potentially create original math word problems, science examples, and non-fiction texts that connect to student interests while also being written at a student's reading level. Students will also be able to interact with the A.I. like a tutor. They'll ask questions and clarify misunderstandings. All of this will happen without the need for a teacher.

While there might be a time and place for such adaptive learning programs, this feels like yet another iteration of the promise that a machine can perfectly personalize learning. I've seen this promise play out with video cassettes, laser discs, interactive CD roms, one-to-one computers, and the previously mentioned adaptive learning intervention systems. This is the promise of Techno Futurism.

What if we began with a human-centered view of personalized learning and then considered ways that we could use A.I. to augment rather than replace the human element?

USING A.I. WITHIN PERSONALIZED LEARNING

At its core, personalized learning focuses on empowering students with voice and choice. Consider what this might look like with a choice menu. Traditionally, choice menus allow students to choose how they will present what they are learning. It's a great first step for students who aren't used to having as much voice and choice in their learning.

While choice menus are great, here's a variation on the choice menu that goes beyond choosing topics and toward student ownership of the learning targets and resources. Here's what it looks like:

Learning Targets Choose 1-2 learning targets that you haven't mastered	Resources Choose 1-3 resources that you will use to learn about the content	Product Choose how you will demonstrate the mastery of the content
Example: I can identify how animals adapt to their habitats I can explain how natural selection works		

Students decide either the topics, concepts, or skills and then choose their own resources and strategies before ultimately creating their final product. I found that this worked well in the following contexts:

- Early on in a unit when students need to acquire more background knowledge and understand concepts at a deeper level
- Toward the end of the unit when students need targeted intervention
- When completing standards that don't work as well with project-based learning or design thinking
- In the moments when there is a time crunch, and they don't have as much time to search for resources
- If you are just making the leap into student-driven learning and you want to start with something that builds on student choice but doesn't require a massive project

Here's where the A.I. becomes a useful tool. You begin with your own standards but then you can use A.I. generators to develop written examples of non-fiction texts that help students master the learning targets. You can then find examples of online videos or images that might be useful as well. But you can also use generative A.I. to create handouts for skill practice or vocabulary work. As you plan your choice menu, you can combine online resources with A.I. generated resources for that second column (resources). You can also use the A.I. to change reading levels, emphasize key vocabulary, or incorporate a student's cultural assets.

When having students demonstrate their knowledge, teachers can select assignments and design rubrics using the A.I. tools. In the case of the science example, students would select the learning targets (which could be labeled and color-coded) and then click on the hyperlinked resources. After re-learning these concepts, students then share their learning in a video demonstration, a podcast, or a slideshow. For each of those options, they would have a hyperlink to an assignment page with directions and a rubric that you initially generate via A.I. and then modify to meet the needs of your students.

Notice that this is similar to the adaptive learning program mentioned before. However, instead of having a computer choosing the options, students get to decide. Similarly, the teacher can curate the resources and modify the assignments rather than depend on the A.I. for every aspect of the choice menu. While this choice menu example is individual, you might have students work with partners or small groups.

Here, the A.I. works on the back end, but the process is more social and human. It resembles an adaptive learning program, but it taps into teacher expertise (as the curator) and student agency in making decisions. In other words, it's human-driven and A.I.-informed.

USING A.I. TO DESIGN LEVELED READING

Sometimes personalized learning is less about students choosing their own topics and more about helping students access the learning in a way where the skill level is just above the learning task.

Imagine you are teaching about industrialization for a seventh-grade social studies class. You want to have a class Socratic Seminar asking the question, "Was the Industrial Revolution an overall negative or positive thing for our world?"

You might begin with a review of the Industrial Revolution. You could start with front-loaded vocabulary using A.I.-generated vocabulary and definitions connected to public domain images (or even A.I.-generated images). From there, you might review what students have already learned about the Industrial Revolution. But before doing your Socratic Seminar, your students complete a quick reading on the pros, cons, and lasting impact of this era.

In this moment, you could start with key points you'd like to cover and then have a generative A.I. create a text written at the 7th Grade reading level. It's not a bad start but it's a little boring, so you edit the text and punch it up with some humor, some bizarre examples, and a few things you think the A.I. missed. From there, the A.I. chatbot can create a leveled reading ranging from 3rd Grade to 7th Grade. Now every student can access the text at a level that matches their fluency level. After reading the text, students jot down specific questions they want to ask in the Socratic Seminar. Finally, students engage in the Socratic Seminar.

Notice that this approach treats A.I. as a learning tool. The process is messy, human, and inherently social. Instead of sitting at a table with headphones and a computer, students engage in a dynamic Socratic Seminar. You're using A.I. as a tool to make learning more accessible without abandoning the authentic human element. In the next chapter, we'll take a deeper journey into this idea of accessibility as we explore what it might look like to use A.I. for supports and scaffolds.

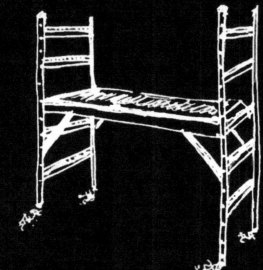

CHAPTER 11

INCORPORATING ARTIFICIAL INTELLIGENCE INTO SCAFFOLDS AND SUPPORTS

We all have things that we can independently but other things that are impossible for us to do. Not to brag but I'm pretty good at loading a dishwasher. On the other hand, I can't slam dunk a basketball. However, there are also certain things in a middle zone that you can't do on your own *quite yet*, but you can accomplish them with a little help. You might need help from a teacher, a peer group, or a resource. With proper training, hours of practice, and a trampoline, I could eventually slam dunk a basketball. Maybe. Okay, probably not.

Vygotsky described this middle space as the Zone of Proximal Development (ZPD).[93] Here's how ZPD works. At the center, you have the things you can do on your own. On the outside, you have the things you cannot do. But in this middle zone you have the Zone of Proximal Development, which are the things you can do with guidance and support.

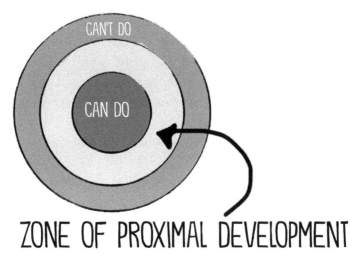

ZONE OF PROXIMAL DEVELOPMENT

In 1976, Jerome Bruner applied Vygotsky's theory to the K-12 educational setting with the concept of scaffolding.[94] Here, educators provide supports, called scaffolds, to help students master the learning. Then, like the scaffolds in a building, teachers pull back the supports as students master the knowledge.

At this point, the ZPD grows outward as students master new knowledge with new scaffolds. As an educator, you might also use

A.I. for this scaffolding process. It could be as simple as an algorithm with "recommended tutorials" for students who are struggling. You might use it to design scaffolds from scratch or to modify existing ones. But for something more intensive, students might use generative A.I. as a type of tutor with a back-and-forth question-and-answer.

USING A.I. TUTORS

With an A.I. tutor, students can submit their work and get immediate feedback and instructions. Other times, students ask the chatbot a question and receive an explanation. Students can then ask follow-up questions in a conversational style. While I see some promise in this type of intervention, we need to think critically about how these systems work. Here are seven questions to consider before implementing these types of A.I. tutoring systems.

1. What are the factual inaccuracies of the bot?

If you've ever spent time giving ChatGPT a set of math prompts, you might notice how inaccurate it tends to be with certain procedural math. The generative A.I. nails complex math conceptual questions but sometimes struggles with basic computations. So, it might do a quality job explaining differential equations but fail when provided a basic two-step equation.

This continues to improve with the newest updates, but it remains an issue. As we move forward in using A.I. tutoring tools, we need to recognize that factual inaccuracies will occur. Generative A.I. uses massive data sets that include misinformation. The machine learning will occasionally come to inaccurate conclusions. In some cases, it's a matter of a poorly worded command prompt (you ask the A.I. a vague question) but other times, there are inaccuracies from the larger data set the A.I. is processing within its neural network.

As we think about using A.I. as a form of tutoring, we need to identify what misinformation might exist. This doesn't mean we abandon A.I. tutoring altogether. After all, human tutors might teach a skill poorly or explain a concept incorrectly. I sometimes cringe at the mistakes I made as a social studies teacher where I later learned I had certain facts wrong relating to historical events. The key here is that we teach students to recognize that an A.I. tutor will make mistakes.

2. What are the biases within the A.I.?

Every form of A.I. contains some biases (remember the example of Tay?). If an educational technology company presents a new A.I. tutoring system, we need to know how the company is actively identifying the bias within the original data. We need transparency regarding how companies are adjusting the algorithms in response to the biases of their A.I. systems.

3. What is the contextual understanding of the A.I.?

In other words, how well would a virtual tutor understand the school and its context? There's always an element of context that's critical to helping students connect the learning to prior knowledge. The best human tutors know how to contextualize the information for students to ensure that they can connect it to their prior knowledge. This includes a student's cultural assets. Which leads to the next question . . .

4. What is the cultural understanding of the A.I.?

Every time I've met with someone who has an adaptive learning program, I ask, "How does the A.I. use culturally sustaining practices?" Often the answer is vague and occasionally even dismissive. However, all learning is rooted in the context of culture. It shapes how we interpret information and organize our thinking. When we treat an A.I. tutor as culturally agnostic, we make the false assumption that there is a "neutral" form of learning that doesn't connect to cultural values and practices.

5. Has the A.I. been trained on human psychology?

I'm concerned with the potential for learned helplessness and dependence on A.I. as a tutoring tool. If we want students to develop resilience, they need to experience productive struggle. I have yet to see an A.I. tutoring platform that incorporates this productive struggle in a meaningful way.

Consider the way the A.I. provides feedback. If an A.I. program starts praising a student's natural ability ("you are an excellent reader") would this accidentally encourage a fixed mindset?[95] If the A.I. uses overly blunt language, would it lead to a drop in student self-efficacy or would it help students gain a more accurate view of their learning?

These are hard questions that psychologists explore on a regular basis. I spent two years exploring the research on motivation and efficacy for my dissertation. I wrestled with complex of questions as I attempted to understand the relationship between Self Determination Theory and ideas like mindset, resilience, and self-efficacy. Even now, I am well-aware of just how little I understand about this topic. We need to know whether it can have a deep, nuanced view of human psychology as it interacts with students.

6. Has the A.I. been trained on human development?

Decades ago, media critic Neil Postman warned about the disappearance of childhood when children use technology designed for adults.[96] If we incorporate A.I. tutoring tools, I want to know how exactly the tools adapts to the developmental needs of students. If you hired a human tutor, you would likely ask what experience that person had working with children of a certain age range. The same is true of A.I. tutors.

7. What is the educational foundation of the A.I. system?

In other words, does this tutoring approach focus on an Information Processing view of learning? A Constructivist view? A Connectivist view? A Social Learning view? If I were a school hiring a math tutor, I would ask, "What is your approach to math pedagogy?" In the same way, we need to ask educational technology companies,

"What is the pedagogical foundation behind the tutoring you provide?"

There is real promise in A.I. for tutoring purposes. Unlike previous
adaptive learning programs, generative A.I. is interactive and dynamic. Students can ask their own questions and interact in a way that
feels human. However, we need to ensure that educational technology companies are asking key questions relating to culture, context,
pedagogy, and human psychology.

In this respect, I've been encouraged by the Khan Academy. In
interviewing Sal Khan on my podcast, I was struck by the intentionality
they had with issues of bias, human development, and aligning the
A.I. to learning theory as they developed Khanmigo.My hope is that
other leaders in the educational technology sector will pay close attention to the human element as they design A.I. tools for K-12
students.

In the upcoming years, teachers will play a vital role in screening
these technology tools. We will need to ask those previously mentioned seven questions to understand how the A.I. tutors will impact
our students. But we will also continue designing the scaffolds that
help students access the content we teach. The good news is we can
use A.I. tools to design these scaffolds.

USING A.I. FOR PERSONALIZED SUPPORTS

Consider how you might help a student who experiences executive dysfunction and has a hard time completing work. A student with executive dysfunction might have difficulty with tasks that require planning, problem-solving, decision-making, and goal setting. This student might struggle with time management and organization.

Here's where the A.I. might help. With guidance and support, students might use generative A.I. to help with goal setting. In the reading intervention example from the previous chapter, an A.I. might be helpful in setting reading endurance or silent reading fluency goals. Students could then track their own goals using an online form.

Here's an example with silent reading endurance. I took the initial A.I.-generated goals and I modified these to create more "early wins" at the start and then progress toward something harder later.

Week 1:
Day 1: Read silently for 3-5 minutes
Day 2: Read silently for 5 minutes
Day 3: Read silently for 6 minutes
Day 4: Read silently for 6 minutes
Day 5: Read silently for 6 minutes

Week 2:
Day 6: Read silently for 7 minutes
Day 7: Read silently for 7 minutes
Day 8: Read silently for 8 minutes
Day 9: Read silently for 9 minutes
Day 10: Read silently for 10 minutes

Another example might be breaking down a complex task into something with sub-tasks. Here the can A.I. to break down the directions into a checklist with more specific directions. The teacher can then modify the initial checklist to personalize the scaffold for an individual student. Consider an assignment where a student needs to create a Google Document used for research on the Mayans. Many students can create the document from scratch and immediately get to work. But some students might be overwhelmed with where to start. I created a checklist using generative A.I. and then added a few "early wins" to create the sense of momentum with the checklist.

- o Make sure you have your computer out and it's ready to go.
- o Look at your surroundings and make sure you don't have any distractions.
- o Turn to your shoulder partner and explain what you will be doing. Use the frame "I will ask questions about _____ and record my answers in _____."
- o Go to Google Docs by typing "docs.google.com" in the address bar at the top of your web browser and pressing the "Enter" key.
- o Click the blue "Blank" button in the middle of the screen to create a new document.
- o Give your document a name by typing it the "Document Title" box at the top left-hand side of the screen. Your title should be "Mayan Civilization Q&A"
- o To share your document with someone else, click the blue "Share" button in the top right corner of the screen.
- o Type the teacher's name and the email address will pop up. Choose whether you want them to be able to make changes, add comments, or just view the document. Share the document with your teacher.
- o Click the blue "Send" button to share the document.
- o To add a table to your document, click on the "Table" button at the top of the screen.
- o Choose how many rows and columns you want your table to have by clicking on the boxes in the grid. Look at the example on the board. You should have 2 columns and 2 rows.
- o Once you've chosen the number of rows and columns you want, click on the grid to insert your table into your document.
- o Write question on the top left-hand side of the table and answer on the right-hand side. Look at the board for your example.
- o Now you can start working on your document by typing in text or adding information to the table.

Notice that for some students with executive function challenges, this checklist might be too detailed. They might need a video or a checklist with fewer steps and a .gif showing how to do each step. But for others, this might be the exact type of task breakdown they need.

You know your students best. The A.I. creates an initial scaffold that you, as the educators, aids, and specialists can modify.

This is just one example of how you might use A.I. to generate structures and scaffolds for neurodiverse students. Here are a few more ideas:

- Providing additional handouts to facilitate task-analysis and executive function
- Using A.I. to help schedule small groups
- Using A.I. speech recognition software as an assistive technology to help students with writing
- Using A.I. image generators to help students who need a more concrete example of what they are learning in class
- Designing targeted skill practice. For example, you might use a chatbot to generate word problems for students who struggle with 2-step equations, or you might use it to create a high-interest non-fiction text at a student's reading with sample questions
- Using A.I. to modify assignments to reduce cognitive load (fewer steps) while encouraging students to still access the grade level content.
- Using A.I. to reduce the amount of work while still maintaining a high challenge level. For example, a student with dyscalculia might need fewer problems but can still master the math content at the same grade level.

None of these supports should replace the goals within an Individualized Education Plan (IEP). We don't want to replace educators with algorithms. We can, however, use the A.I. as a starting place for designing more personalized scaffolds and supports. Here, the A.I. platform saves time and makes the differentiation process more feasible for teachers. It works like an assistant to create something general that you can then modify based on your own expertise and knowledge of students.

USING A.I. TO GENERATE LANGUAGE SCAFFOLDS

Previously, we examined how to help provide supports for neurodiverse students. But what about students who are learning English as a speaker of another language (ELL, ESL, ESOL students)? We can use A.I. as an initial starting place for creating language supports. These include:

- **Front-loading vocabulary:** you can use A.I. to identify some of the Tier 2 and Tier 3 vocabulary that students might need to master. While you'll still need to create a list of vocabulary yourself (and rely on student feedback) the A.I. can be a great starting place. I've found that certain chatbots do a great job defining vocabulary in simple terms and even coming up with example sentences. If you couple this with an A.I. image generator, you can save time in generating front-loaded vocabulary, handouts, and slideshows.
- **Providing translation help**: While it still works best to partner students with someone who is multilingual, A.I. translators have come a long way. The dynamic aspects of an A.I. bot allow students to interact with the content in their native language while also being exposed to content in English. This is especially helpful for students are feeling shy or even scared about speaking a new language in front of their peers.
- **Providing leveled sentence stems:** This remains a weaker area for A.I. but I am noticing significant improvements in A.I.-generated sentence stems, sentence frames, and clozes. The key is in making the prompts specific and clear.
- **Using visuals within the project to help facilitate language development:** As A.I.-generated visual art continues to improve, we can potentially create additional visuals that can aid with accessing English.

- **Assess language proficiency:** A.I. can work as a formative assessment tool by analyzing a student's speech or writing. This can be particularly useful in assessing language learners who may not have access to a native speaker or who are learning in a remote setting.
- **Language practice:** Students can provide the A.I. chatbot with the directions to engage in a language role-playing conversation. They can set the purpose, location, and fictional person they want to A.I. to pretend to be. Then, they can practice English with the chatbot.

Notice that a teacher can begin with these A.I.-generated supports but then modify them to suit their context. Teachers might even invite students to help with this modification process. This then frees teachers up to pay attention to a students' affective filter and finding ways to reduce fear and anxiety.

I've noticed that ELL teachers tend to spend a significant amount of time designing supports and scaffolds. Meanwhile, many ELL students in a non-ELL classroom fail to receive certain supports they need. If we can leverage A.I. to save time in designing scaffolds, we can help students access the content while improving in their language development.

A.I. WON'T REPLACE THE NEED FOR TEACHERS TO DIFFERENTIATE INSTRUCTION. BUT IT WILL MAKE DIFFERENTIATION MORE FEASIBLE.

STUDENTS NEED PRODUCTIVE STRUGGLE

AVOIDING LEARNED HELPLESSNESS

"I just want you to know that three of our exceptional learners were in tears today. We were working on the STEAM projects, and I thought I provided the right supports but . . ."

"Good," our special education teacher interrupted.

"What do you mean?" I asked.

"They came into their next class and told me all about it," she said.

"I'm confused," I admitted.

"They didn't tell me about the tears. They told me about the struggles they faced but they also told me all about what they did to get their solar ovens to work," she answered.

"I feel bad, though," I pointed out.

"You shouldn't feel bad at all. Look, they cried because they cared. Do any of your other students cry during projects?"

"Sometimes," I admitted.

"The same should be true of students with learning differences. They need to experience productive struggle. A lot of them have developed learned helplessness. Teachers with the best of intentions have given them the answers instead of giving a scaffold," she said.

"You really think it's okay that they cried?" I asked.

"My goal has been to get them to be self-directed. I want them to be their own advocates. But I also want them to do so in a way that fosters resilience."

Learned helplessness refers to a psychological phenomenon where students develop a belief that they are incapable of performing certain tasks or learning specific skills. They may become passive, disengaged, or unmotivated in the learning process.

This can happen when a teacher gives too much help too early and fails to encourage productive struggle. It can also happen when there's a lack of support or an overly critical environment. When students repeatedly experience failure or perceive a task as too difficult, they may begin to feel that their efforts are futile.

As we implement A.I. for scaffolding, we need to ensure that it doesn't short-circuit productive struggle. If students get immediate help with any question they have, this might develop into a form of learned helplessness.

As we think about designing supports for students, it will ultimately be about the implementation rather than merely the design of the scaffolds we use. Ultimately, teachers have the relational knowledge to provide the necessary scaffolding to help students master the standards. A.I. simply makes this more feasible.

EMPOWERING STUDENTS TO USE A.I. FOR SUPPORTS

I had a student ask for the transcript from our class Zoom session. He used the chatbot to delete the time stamps and translate it to Spanish. As a dual language student, he likes using both languages as he wrestles with ideas and compares the transcription to his notes in both languages.

I share this story because every time there's a new technology and people are scared about cheating, I always ask, "How are people using this to scaffold their own learning?"

In other words, how might an exceptional learner use this? How might an English Language Learner use this? How might someone who hasn't had the same advantages use this? Because what might seem to some as a "chance to cheat" might be a game-changer for someone else.

As educators, we can empower students to self-select the scaffolds they use. So, while you might make modifications for specific students (like the previously mentioned checklists or modified assignments) you might also have a bank of different tutorials and scaffolds that students can access if they need additional help. These supports should be available to all students. This approach embodies Universal Design for Learning.[97]

Built around cognitive neuroscience, UDL is an inclusive educational framework that seeks to remove barriers while also keeping the learning challenging for all students. A UDL approach includes certain paradigm shifts:

- From a deficit mindset to neurodiversity
- From singular accommodations to universally accessible scaffolds and supports
- From a teacher-centric view to a student-centered approach centered on student agency

In the 1990's, Dr. David Rose and the Center for Applied Special Technology (CAST) articulated the three UDL principals:[98]

1. **Multiple Means of Representation**: Presenting information in different ways (like text, images, videos, or audio).
2. **Multiple Means of Action and Expression:** Allowing students to engage with and demonstrate their knowledge and skills in various ways (such as through writing, speaking, multimedia, or hands-on activities).
3. **Multiple Means of Engagement:** Fostering motivation and interest in learning by offering choices, using relevant content, encouraging collaboration, and employing strategies to keep students engaged.

Note that students should be empowered to select the scaffolds and supports they need. The focus here is on their own agency and autonomy. Students are empowered throughout all three UDL principles.

With A.I., Universal Design is more feasible. We might use A.I.-driven virtual labs or simulations to help students solve challenging problems. We can provide students with options for the media format of their finished products. The students can then leverage A.I. for their creative work. We can use A.I. to design better projects and choice menus. We might even provide access to A.I. tutors.

Universal Design for Learning embraces the diversity of all learners so that all students are empowered to become self-directed problem-solvers and lifelong learners – the very skills they will need as they navigate the maze of an uncertain future.

Ultimately, we can't predict how A.I. will change learning. We can observe how it is changing creativity, information literacy, personalized learning, and assessment. But we can't predict what this will look like in a decade.

What can do is empower our students to be adaptable as they experience these changes. We can help them see how they can use A.I. as a tool to make the learning more accessible – whether that's with scaffolds and supports or through machine learning for feedback.

Meanwhile, we can help students develop the deeply human skills they will as they navigate this changing landscape. In our next section, we will explore what these changes mean for specific subject areas.

PART THREE

HOW WILL ARTIFICIAL INTELLIGENCE CHANGE EACH CONTENT AREA?

In Part 2, we explored how A.I. is changing the landscape of every aspect of learning. But what about actual content areas and disciplines? Machine learning will change the way we engage with history, compose writing, make art, and do math. It will impact classes like heath and PE and world languages. It will transform what CTE programs look like as we prepare students for the maze of an uncertain future.

A.I. will continue to change every field of study. But it might also change the way we view the idea of a content area. Traditionally, schools have treated subjects as stand-alone disciplines. English Language Arts is where you read, write, and study literature. Social studies class is where you learn history, economics, civics, and geography. Math is where you learn algebraic thinking, statistics, and problem-solving.

However, we also know that every one of these subjects connects to other disciplines. Historical knowledge informs our understanding of classic literature while the ability to read and write impacts our understanding of history. It's not surprising that schools have combined ELA and social studies into a larger humanities block. Meanwhile, the recent popularity of STEAM (Science, Technology, Engineering, Art, Math) points to the reality that science isn't merely a singular field.

The future of learning will likely be interdisciplinary. We will need to shift from silos, where students work in a single subject, and toward rhizomes.

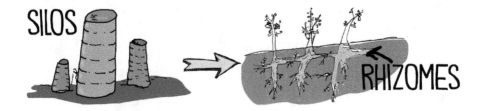

A rhizome is a type of underground stem that grows horizontally, sending out shoots from its nodes. Think of it like a giant web where that's interconnected instead of a traditional plant with roots that lead up to a stem. With a rhizome, there is no single, centralized starting place. This decentralized approach allows plants to spread into new areas in seemingly creative ways. Rhizomes can store nutrients and energy for the plant and can survive harsh conditions like drought or fire. Examples of plants that have rhizomes include ginger, bamboo, and some species of grasses. If our students need to navigate the maze, their learning will need to be rhizomatic, with subject areas and disciplines connecting to one another. This approach will help students grow resilient while sparking innovation and creativity.

Innovation often occurs when we use knowledge, skills, and tools from one discipline in a different domain. So, statistics impacts the way we understand history and geography. Scientific tools have helped us understand ancient history. Psychologists challenged some of the biggest economic assumptions in developing behavioral economics. Often, inventors borrow ideas from one domain and apply those in a new area. James Dyson borrowed ideas from mill technology (he had helped design an industrial cyclone tower) and applied it to vacuum cleaner design. This is the type of interdisciplinary thinking our students will engage in as they navigate the maze.

As you read the following chapters, I encourage you to ask, "What does this mean for my students?" You might teach high school history but something in the section on math or science spark your thinking about A.I. and your students' projects. You might teach fourth grade (all subjects) and think of new ways to connect the subject areas as you go. But also, if you find a particular chapter to be irrelevant to your context, feel free to skip it. This is a map and you decide your own journey!

CHAPTER 12
INTEGRATING ARTIFICIAL INTELLIGENCE INTO MATHEMATICS

"There's no way an A.I. can actually solve complex math problems just by looking at it," a teacher said with his arms folded.

"Trust me. Just watch," our math department chair replied. He opened his browser to Wolfram Alpha and typed in an example problem from our textbook.

Collectively we gasped as the results appeared on the interactive whiteboard.

"That's the right answer," a teacher said.

"It has the graph, too," another teacher said, pointing to the plot points.

Another teacher mumbled an expletive under her breath.

"Check this out," our department chair said, clicking on a button. Suddenly, the step-by-step directions appeared.

"What does this mean?" the first teacher asked.

At this point, we engaged in a hard conversation about the future of math education. Some wanted to ban the site entirely. Others hoped that it wouldn't catch on. We could simply ignore it. But there was another teacher who disagreed.

"What if we used it? What if it provides accurate, real-time, feedback that kids will need? One of the hardest things about being a math teacher is giving quick corrective feedback. We end up with students practicing things incorrectly for days before they take a test. This could be a feedback machine."

"I think that's wishful thinking," another teacher said. "Kids are going to use it to cheat. They'll type in their homework, copy the answers, and won't be prepared for the test."

"I agree. I want it blocked," another teacher chimed in.

"Think of it this way," the optimistic teacher began, "We already run into the problem of recipe-based math. Kids look at the example on the board and they think it must solve it in the precise way the teacher did. They get anxious about doing it wrong. They treat the teacher's example as if it's a recipe."

The skeptic nodded, "I see your point. Maybe we ask students to use this Wolfgang Alphabet robot thingy and then they see if they can find another way to solve it. Maybe we incorporate it into the learning. It becomes a partner where they can compare math strategies."

This was over a decade ago. Since then, we've seen apps like Photo Math take this concept in another direction, with the ability to take a photo of a math problem and solve it step-by-step directions. While the concerns about A.I. and math have been valid, math teachers have already spent over a decade finding strategies for teaching math in an age of A.I. And yet, we often focus these conversations on the procedural aspects of math. Meanwhile, generative A.I. can be a great tool for conceptual understanding.

USING A.I. FOR CONCEPTUAL UNDERSTANDING

One of the hardest things for a student in Statistics is the notion of a p-value. What exactly does it mean and what exactly does it look like? There are some great online examples with videos and visuals. I'm partial to the Crash Course video series.

However, sometimes students need a little bit of extra help and a chatbot can provide a conversational approach to help clarify the concept of a p-value. A student might begin by asking, "What is a p-value?" The A.I. gives a pretty good answer.

A p-value is a statistical measure used to determine the likelihood that an observed effect or result could have occurred by chance. In other words, it measures the probability of obtaining a result as extreme or more extreme than the one observed if the null hypothesis were true.

The null hypothesis is a statement that assumes there is no significant difference or relationship between two or more groups or variables being studied. The p-value is typically expressed as a number between 0 and 1, with a smaller p-value indicating a stronger evidence against the null hypothesis.

If the p-value is less than a pre-determined threshold, typically 0.05, the result is considered statistically significant. This means that there is strong evidence against the null hypothesis, and the observed effect or relationship is likely not due to chance. Conversely, if the p-value is greater than the threshold, the result is not considered statistically significant, and the null hypothesis cannot be rejected.

It is important to note that p-values alone do not provide evidence in favor of any particular hypothesis or explanation, and should be interpreted in conjunction with other factors, such as effect size and study design, when drawing conclusions from statistical analysis.

However, as I look at this, it's a bit complicated. If I were a 17-year-old student, I might need a simpler explanation. So, I modify the prompt asking it to explain this to a 15-year-old. Here's the response.

Imagine you and your friend want to find out if a new medicine for a headache really works. To do this, you give the medicine to a group of people with headaches and another group a placebo (a fake medicine). After some time, you compare the results between the two groups to see if the real medicine works better.

But you also want to make sure that the difference you see between the two groups is not just due to chance. To help you with this, you use something called a p-value.

The p-value is like a score that tells you how likely it is that the difference you see between the two groups is due to chance. If the p-value is low (usually less than 0.05), it means that there is a very small chance that the difference is just due to chance. If the p-value is high, it means that the difference could just be due to chance.

So, when you see a low p-value, you can feel more confident that the new medicine really works better than the placebo. But it's important to remember that a low p-value doesn't mean that the medicine will work for everyone or that it's the best option for every headache. It's just one way to help scientists figure out if something works or not.

The second answer is easier to understand. It's written in a simpler verb tense with less content vocabulary. Overall, the language feels more casual ("like a score that tells you"). While it's true we need students to use precise content vocabulary and complex academic language, in this moment, the student needs to develop a deeper understanding of p-value and that requires simplified language.

Next, the student asks, "How do I know if a p-value is reasonable?" Here's the answer.

A p-value is a way to measure how likely it is that the results of a study happened just by chance. A p-value of less than 0.05 means that the results are unlikely to have happened by chance, and are usually considered "significant." But, just because a p-value is significant, it doesn't mean that the results are important or meaningful. Other things, like how big the effect is, or how the study was done, also need to be considered.

Different fields of study have different standards for what is considered a significant p-value, and those standards should be taken into account when interpreting results. Overall, a p-value is just one piece of information that helps researchers figure out if their results are reliable, but they need to look at other things too to fully understand what their study means.

Now a student might be thinking, "I can see how p-values are used in experimental design. It's starting to click. But what about correlational studies?" Here, the answer could be more technical:

P-values can be used in non-experimental and correlational studies as well as in experimental studies. In fact, p-values are often used in correlational studies to test the significance of the relationship between two variables. In non-experimental studies, researchers observe and measure existing differences or relationships between groups or variables, rather than manipulating them as in an experimental study. In such studies, p-values can still be used to evaluate the likelihood of observing the results by chance.

In correlational studies, researchers examine the relationship between two or more variables without manipulating them. P-values can be used to determine the significance of the correlation coefficient, which measures the strength and direction of the relationship between variables.

Having a hypothesis is not a requirement for using p-values. However, the use of p-values typically requires the formulation of a null hypothesis, which assumes that there is no significant difference or relationship between the groups or variables being studied. The alternative hypothesis, which is the opposite of the null hypothesis, states that there is a significant difference or relationship.

That might be exactly what the student needs. Or again, the student could ask for it to be explained in a way that a 15-year-old could understand:

> P-values can be used in studies where researchers are trying to understand relationships between things, like how one variable affects another. This can be done in experiments, where researchers control the variables they're studying, or in studies where they just observe what's already happening.
>
> In both cases, researchers come up with a hypothesis, which is an educated guess about what they expect to find. They then use p-values to figure out how likely it is that their results could have happened by chance, and whether their hypothesis is supported by their data.
>
> While p-values can be a useful tool for scientists, they should always be used alongside other information and considerations to fully understand what their study means.

Notice the ease of getting clarifying questions answered. Now imagine this student is a sports fan. She wants to know how it might be used in basketball. So, she asks for five examples from basketball:

1. To determine whether a player's free throw shooting percentage has improved from one season to the next. Researchers could calculate a p-value to see if the difference in percentages is statistically significant, indicating whether the player's improvement is likely due to more than just chance.
2. To test whether taller players tend to have higher scoring averages than shorter players. Researchers could use a correlation coefficient and p-value to determine if there is a significant relationship between height and scoring, and if so, whether height is a strong predictor of scoring.
3. To evaluate whether a team's win-loss record is better at home or away. Researchers could use a t-test to determine if the difference in win percentage between home and away games is statistically significant, indicating whether the team truly performs better in one setting over the other.

4. To examine whether a team's three-point shooting accuracy varies significantly across different game situations (e.g., when leading vs. when trailing). Researchers could use an ANOVA and p-value to determine if there are significant differences in shooting percentage across game situations, indicating whether teams might adjust their strategies depending on the score.

5. To determine whether a new basketball shoe design has an impact on players' performance. Researchers could use a hypothesis test and p-value to compare the performance of players wearing the new shoes versus players wearing the old shoes, and determine whether any differences are statistically significant, indicating whether the new shoe design actually provides a performance advantage.

Unfortunately, the chatbot can't give this student a visual of the p-value. This will likely be available in the near future. However, when asked how to calculate the p-value using a spreadsheet, the directions are clear and concrete.

Notice that the focus here is on a deeper understanding of a challenging mathematical concept. While we tend to think of A.I. as a tool for the procedural aspects of math, this gave-and-take conversation is a snapshot into the conceptual understanding that goes into a subject like statistics.

Currently, generative A.I. still struggles with the procedural aspects of math.[99] It's a language learning model that hasn't been trained on procedural aspects of math, However, it can be a great tool for helping students understand the context of math by generating instant real-world examples.

And yet, we also need to recognize the limitations in asking A.I. to provide authentic contexts for math. There's a danger in generative A.I. creating pseudo-context, or a fake context, for a math concept. We see this issue of pseudo-context in certain math textbooks, where the word problems seem boring and irrelevant.

DESIGNING BETTER STORY PROBLEMS

When I taught eighth grade math, we had a word problem in our math book that asked students to imagine that they were a catcher and needed to use the Pythagorean Theorem to figure out the distance from home plate to second base before throwing a runner out.

"Couldn't you just Google that?" a student asked.

"Why would you?" another student chimed in. "Every Major League catcher knows the distance is 127 feet and 4 inches. By the time you Googled it, the runner would be at third base."

This word problem is an example of what Dan Meyer refers to as pseudo-context. [100] It's what happens when students use math in a way that doesn't reflect an authentic context. Students are less engaged when they solve irrelevant and inauthentic problems. As humans, we are naturally driven to solve problems. But if the context is artificial, we disengage.

If we take that same example problem from the math book, we can give it a makeover. This time, it's the day after the state championship game. The opposing team accuses the home team of reducing the distance between home plate and second base to throw players out at second. The catcher has a great "pop time" and an extra foot could make a huge difference. According to them, the base is closer to the plate but still 90 feet from first to second. The curvature on the pitcher's mound makes it impossible to measure from home to second. How do we solve it? Can you prove the home team didn't cheat?

STUDENTS DON'T

HATE

WORD PROBLEMS.
THEY HATE
BAD STORIES

Notice the difference between the two separate word problems. Consider how the sense of conflict changes and how the notion of authenticity varies. The problem is more challenging. Students would need to prove whether the allegedly modified diamond is actually two right triangles. It's still not a perfect word problem but it is more authentic. Generative A.I. sometimes struggles with authenticity and context. I asked a chatbot to generate a word problem comparing two linear equations. This was the response:

> A clothing store sells two types of t-shirts: basic t-shirts and premium t-shirts. The basic t-shirts sell for $15 each and the premium t-shirts sell for $20 each. Last month, the store sold a total of 200 t-shirts and made $3400 in sales. If the store sold twice as many basic t-shirts as premium t-shirts, how many of each type of t-shirt did they sell?

Notice the inherent pseudo-context within this problem. Why would the store know that they had sold twice as many basic t-shirts than premium t-shirts but not know the actual amount of each shirt sold? It just doesn't make sense from an accounting standpoint. This also doesn't factor in the question of profit or operating costs. There's no tension and no conflict. If we're going for t-shirts, a better option might be the following:

> You have been chosen to run the merchandise for an up-and-coming YouTube influencer. This influencer currently uses a print-on-demand store that charges $14.00 per t-shirt. She has hired you to launch the new merchandise store. You currently have two different options for the t-shirts. The first is a start-up cost of $9,000 to get the screen print set up but the cost per shirt is only $3.60 with free shipping. The second vendor gives you a bid for a $2,500 up-front cost and $9.75 with a cost of $1.20 shipping per shirt. Which vendor should this YouTube influencer use if she's selling just a few shirts? Which vendor should she use if she's selling a lot of shirts? At what point would this influencer want to switch vendors?

This option is more realistic. It's the type of predictive accounting where people use linear equations in real life. Plus, it connects to something people know – vendors selling merchandise. You could easily take it to the next level by showing a table with the number of shirts being sold each month. Students would then have to identify trends and make predictions based on growth in subscriber counts.

A.I. is great at explaining concepts and even generating examples. But when it comes to authentic context, humans tend to excel. As we think about math in a world of A.I., one of the solutions might be to explore the initial examples that A.I. generates but then bring in the human element to clarify the actual context of the applied mathematics.

USING A.I. AS AN EXAMPLE GENERATOR

While generative A.I. does poorly at designing word problems, chat bots can still help students find example of where they might use the math they are learning in an authentic context. When I asked ChatGPT to generate examples of derivatives in our world, this was the answer:

Derivatives are used in many real-life applications, including finance, physics, engineering, and more. Here are a few examples:

1. Finance: Derivatives are used extensively in finance to manage risk and speculate on future price movements. For example, futures contracts and options contracts are types of derivatives that allow investors to lock in a price for a future transaction. Derivatives are also used in complex financial instruments like mortgage-backed securities and collateralized debt obligations.

2. Physics: Derivatives are used in physics to describe the behavior of physical systems. For example, the derivative of position with respect to time gives us velocity, and the derivative of velocity with respect to time gives us acceleration. These concepts are essential for understanding motion, force, and energy.

3. Engineering: Derivatives are used in engineering to describe the behavior of complex systems. For example, the derivative of pressure with respect to volume gives us the bulk modulus, which is a measure of the resistance of a material to compression. Derivatives are also used in control systems to analyze and design feedback loops.

4. Optimization: Derivatives are used in optimization problems to find the minimum or maximum value of a function. For example, a company

might use derivatives to optimize its production process to minimize costs while maximizing output.

5. Data analysis: Derivatives are used in data analysis to find patterns and trends in data. For example, the derivative of a function that describes the growth of a population over time can help us identify the rate of growth and predict future population sizes.

At this point, it might help to reach out to industry partners and community connections to find out how derivatives are used in contexts outside of school. As a teacher, you could move from the initial ideas generated by A.I. to specific real-world examples offered by engineers, manufacturers, pollsters, or accountants who use the math in their settings.

While the previous example involves high school calculus, what does this mean for elementary school? How do we help students find the authentic context in early elementary school?

It might involve connecting rates and measurements to cooking or to shopping. It might involve exploring 3D shapes as part of a PBL experience of redesigning their school playground. You might give students a challenge of creating the layout for a solar farm to understand arrays.

OUR STUDENTS
WILL NEED TO SOLVE

WICKED

PROBLEMS

Dr. John Spencer

SOLVING WICKED PROBLEMS

I recently worked with a university shifting their engineering program to incorporate a more project-based and problem-based approach. One key takeaway from a survey with industry partners was that their students were great at solving narrow problems. They struggled, however, with "wicked problems."

A "wicked problem" is a term used to describe a complex problem that is difficult to define, understand, and solve. The term was first coined by urban planner Horst Rittel and political scientist Melvin Webber in 1973 to describe social and cultural issues that are resistant to traditional problem-solving methods.[101]

In engineering, wicked problems are the type that don't have one simple solution. Attempts to solve one aspect of the problem may create new issues or unintended consequences in other areas. They require divergent thinking and constant iteration. One industry partner put this way, "University graduates are great at solving problems. But we need people who know how to find problems and look at unintended consequences."

In a world dominated by A.I., where digital modeling and problem-solving will occur at a rapid-fire pace, our students will need to solve wicked problems.

Students might engage with an A.I.-fueled simulation, where their initial decisions create unintended consequences. They would need to ask the right questions, look for the right information, and think divergently as they apply the math they are learning. Here the A.I. could work on the backend to run the simulation, but it might also be a tool they use to gain new understanding, get instant feedback on their work, and view data visualizations.

Meanwhile, students will work in teams as they tackle the problems and develop key human skills like resilience, collaboration, empathy, and divergent thinking. It will be A.I.-informed but human-driven.

IF ARTIFICIAL INTELLIGENCE CAN SOLVE IT, SHOULD STUDENTS STILL LEARN IT?

I walk into the 4th grade classroom and immediately notice the challenge on the board. It looks nothing like my memory of early elementary math class. There are no timed tests. No stacks of worksheets. No rows of desks. They start with a simple question about the best way to fit solar panels on a particular plot of land.

Students work individually at first. They draw pictures and use manipulatives. A few of them write out the algorithm. But then, as they move into teams, they compare strategies. They discuss possible solutions. They advocate for their ideas and ask clarifying questions. Eventually, they land on their ultimate solution.

At this point, the teacher adds a few more details. She has some new challenges they haven't considered. She adds the elements of costs and rate to the challenge. Students now modify their solutions to fit with the new information.

Notice that everything they are doing could be done with A.I. But students need to engage in this type of mathematical thinking if we want them to become problem-solvers, systems thinkers, and collaborators. These are the human skills they will need in a world of A.I.

While this starts as a low-tech exploration activity, students then move on to a simulated conversation with the A.I., who functions as a fictional customer. The students must explain their process and defend their proposal. The A.I. helps guide reflection in a way that feels interactive. It's an extension, rather than replacement, of the hands-on learning they just engaged in.

The next day, students do a mental math exercise followed by direct instruction. They take notes and practice three problems. But they also get immediate feedback on their problems through a generative A.I. "tutor" offering diagnostic help. This lesson is far more traditional, skill-based, and foundational than the previous day's lesson but it will help build their prior knowledge for a problem-based exploration they will do a few days later.

This teacher is avoiding the dead ends of Techno-Futurism and the Lock It and Block It approach. This approach to math helps students develop deeper number sense and numeracy while also improving their problem-solving skills. Students are developing deeper content knowledge but applying it to real-world scenarios in a way that will help them navigate an unpredictable future. This approach to math might just be the foundation that will help our students solve complex problems in the future.

We can't predict how A.I. will change math in the future. But as we think about our A.I. roadmap, we can focus on the human skills students will need as this terrain changes. We can use A.I. as a tool for generating examples, clarifying concepts, and guiding reflection. But we can do so in a way rooted in a human context.

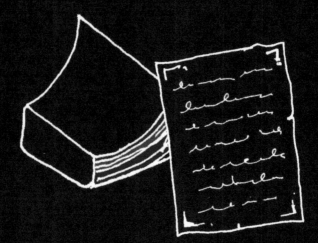

CHAPTER 13
INTEGRATING ARTIFICIAL INTELLIGENCE INTO LANGUAGE ARTS

In December of 2022, I showed ChatGPT to another professor.

"I'm not worried about A.I. in my Humanities courses," she said.

"Not at all?" I asked.

She shook her head. "I know of colleagues who are going back to the blue books and banning devices. Or they're looking into programs that can detect ChatGPT in an essay. But I'm just wondering how we might use this tool to transform the essay."

"What kinds of transformations do you see in the future?"

"It's too early to tell. But I've been down this road before. When I realized students could just download whole essays, I started requiring students to do pre-writing that they turned in to me earlier in the process. I changed to high interest writing prompts that you couldn't find online. Now I see that ChatGPT can generate responses to those prompts and I'm going to think hard about how treat A.I. as a tool. I want to know how it might transform the whole idea of an essay."

Together, we planned out a solution that would include blending together A.I.-generated and student-generated text. It was a reminder that the essay isn't dead, but it is changing. It will continue to evolve in the upcoming years. For now, the use of A.I. is forcing us to ask, "When is A.I. a learning tool and when is it cheating?"

ARTIFICIAL INTELLIGENCE WON'T KILL THE ESSAY.

BUT IT WILL CHANGE IT.

Dr. John Spencer

WHEN IS IT CHEATING?

When I was a new teacher, I had several teachers warn me not to have my students use spellcheck. If we relied too heavily on technology to fix spelling mistakes, students would grow complacent, and their spelling would grow even worse.

That semester, I had students submit a writing sample. I counted the words and the number of spelling errors to find the rate of spelling mistakes. I then had students do a handwritten assessment at the end of the semester. There was a significant decrease in the number of spelling mistakes after using spellcheck. It turned out this tool used for cheating was actually providing students with immediate feedback on their spelling mistakes. Instead of mindlessly clicking on the spellcheck, students were internalizing the feedback.

Spellcheck is now pervasive in writing. What was once a tool for "cheating" is now a tool for writing. This is part of a larger trend of viewing new technology as cheating. Word pressing program were considered cheating compared to re-typing an entire document. Search engines were cheating compared to using card catalogs and microfilm. Automatic citation generators are still considered to be cheating in some academic circles. In math, spreadsheets, calculators, and large data analytics programs (such as SPSS) have been labeled as cheating at various times. Generative A.I. is merely the newest technology that people view as cheating.

EVERY TOOL
WAS ONCE
CONSIDERED
CHEATING

Students have been using A.I. in their writing for the last two decades. We don't tend to think of spellcheck as A.I. But it is a primitive example of a smart algorithm. While spellcheck software is not as advanced as the newer generations of A.I., it still relies on machine learning and pattern recognition to improve its accuracy over time. Some spellcheck software may also use natural language processing techniques to detect contextual errors. If a word is spelled correctly but poorly placed (such as a homonym) or misunderstood, it gets flagged.

Students are already using more advanced A.I. in every phase of the writing process. When doing research, the auto-fill option in Google narrows down the search for students. When typing in a Google Document, the auto-fill option will often complete the sentences for students. As students edit their work, the grammar check offers suggestions for what needs to change. Students might even use an A.I. tool like Grammarly to polish their writing in the editing phase. The A.I. is so thoroughly integrated into the process that it doesn't feel like the A.I. writing is a paper. However, machine learning is already integrated into these aspects of the writing process.

Note that all these tools have been considered cheating at some point. Eventually, these tools become essential elements to the learning and creative processes. And yet, generative A.I. feels different. It's one thing to use A.I. as an editor making suggestions. It's another thing to use generative A.I. to produce the text itself.

So where does that leave us with cheating? When is A.I. simply a tool to enhance learning and when is it co-opting and replacing a vital part of the learning process? Matt Miller conceptualizes it as a continuum from bot-created to human-created.[102]

As Miller describes, "We're going to have to draw a line -- as educators, as schools, even as school districts -- to determine what we're going to allow and what we aren't." [103]

THE FUTURE IS BLENDED

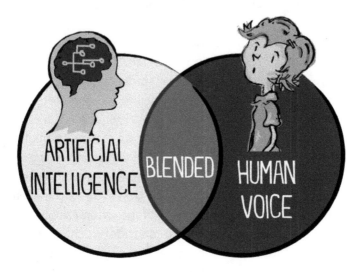

Blended writing is the overlap of human voice and machine learning. This blended approach to writing isn't new. For centuries, we have been using technology to help us write. Many technological historians view writing itself as a form of technology. Certainly, tools like the printing press, typewriter, and computer led to more automation within the writing process. But this overlap was often "human first," with the machine making the editing process faster and more feasible. What's different is that the machine can now do so much more. So, what this mean for the future of writing?

A BLENDED APPROACH TO ESSAY WRITING

This blended approach moves away from the two dead ends of Techno Futurism and Lock It and Block It. Instead, it focuses on using A.I. wisely to enhance the learning while also embracing the human elements.

A blended approach might include a mix of hand-written and A.I.-generated writing. Students can create sketchnotes, drawings and text by hand in a journal. These low-tech options focus on writing as a way of "making learning visible."[104] Afterward, students might use A.I. to clarify misconceptions. From there, they create their own outline but use A.I. to expand it. They might create a first draft but then ask A.I. for feedback. So, there's this ebb and flow between human-generated and A.I.-generated writing. However, the process is human-first with A.I. as a tool to take the writing to the next level.

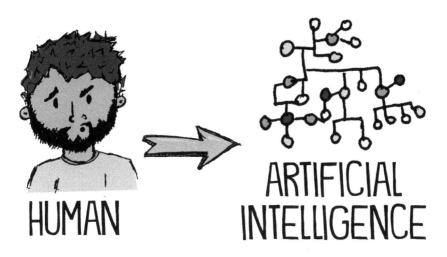

HUMAN → ARTIFICIAL INTELLIGENCE

These same students might take a different approach in another assignment by using a chatbot to generate new ideas as a starting place and then add their own ideas afterward. They might use an A.I.-generated response that they then modify it to provide new insights. Here they might use A.I. as the starting place and add their own unique voice to the finished product. Unlike the previous approach, this blended approach is A.I.-first but modified to become more human.

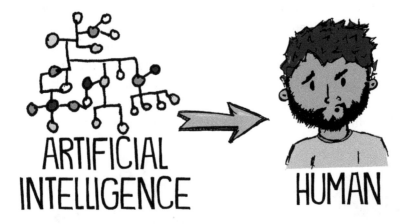

Students can use A.I. wisely by focusing the strengths of both the human and machine learning. Machine learning does well with synthesizing information from multiple sources and generating text that's clear and readable. Machine learning can also help with editing and ideation. Humans do well with voice and tone (especially humor). We understand context and can write with empathy. While both A.I. and humans can write creatively, we are better divergent thinkers.

Let's explore what it looks like to blend together A.I. and human-generated content in each phase of the writing process.

THE BLENDED APPROACH EMBRACES THE STRENGTHS OF BOTH THE HUMAN AND THE MACHINE

PHASE 1:
INITIAL CONCEPTUAL UNDERSTANDING

I sometimes think about this as the pre-pre-writing stage. It's the phase where students access their prior knowledge before asking questions and engaging in research. A blended approach might start with a K-W-L chart on a shared document. Students jot down everything they know about the topic. Next, they write down everything they want to know about the topic. At this point, instead of moving into research, students would use a chatbot to ask questions and learn about the topic.

For this example, a social studies student learning about World War I might have an essay question, "How susceptible are we to having another world war? Could that happen again?"

Students would first do a round robin brainstorm, where they jot down everything they know and want to know in a KWL chart. Then, they would go individually to the A.I. A student might ask the chatbot, "What were the causes of World War I?" This student would then read about militarism, the alliance system, imperialism, and nationalism.

At this point, the student might ask follow-up questions, like "Why would an assassination lead to a whole world at war?" Or perhaps this student feels confused by militarism and asks, "Can you give me examples of militarism?" It could be a random question like, "What did they call World War I before World War II happened?"

Students would then add this information to their KWL chart. The process would be dynamic with the A.I. functioning as an interactive tool for conceptual understanding.

PHASE 2
RESEARCH

In this phase, students would engage in online research by generating questions and finding answers. They might start with an initial set of questions but then amplify it by asking a chatbot to come up with research questions for them. During the online research, they would read articles but also use the chatbot to clarify misunderstandings. Here, the A.I. functions like a group member who can help answer questions but also ask students questions to help guide their understanding.

A student might use the prompt, "Pretend you are a group member doing research with me on World War I. I'm going to ask questions and you can ask me questions as well." Note that this process takes some training for the chatbot. As a teacher, you would need to model how this works. Even then, it can sometimes feel a bit artificial, so group members will need to experiment with prompts as they interact with the chatbot.

A more frequent option would be the take complex text from a primary source and have the chatbot simplify the language. Students can still summarize it but with simpler grammar, they can access the thinking more readily.

Students might work in teams to compare their information and discuss their findings. Students would create a hand-drawn concept maps showing the connections between ideas. But they might use A.I. during this phase to clarify specific words or terms. Notice that this is a human-driven, personalized approach. The A.I. is merely another tool in the research process.

PHASE 3
ORGANIZING IDEAS AND OUTLINING

In this phase, students brainstorm ideas and organize them into a coherent outline. They might do a mind map or organize their ideas with sticky notes. At some point, students would create an initial outline for their essay and then use an A.I. to generate an outline as well. Then, after comparing the two outlines, they would modify their own outline to fill in some of the gaps that the A.I. pointed out. They could also ask the A.I. chatbot for feedback on their original outline. Here, the A.I. functions as a personalized assessment tool. Another option might be to start with an A.I. generated outline and then modify it based on their own preferences.

PHASE 4
WRITING

In this phase, students could take their initial outline and ask for the chatbot to generate the actual text. From here, students modify the text to add their own voice. They write additional sentences using their research chart. Here students add facts and citations that they explain in their own words. The initial chatbot text would be color-coded as black but the human text would be a color of the students' choice.

In some cases, though, students might opt out from using A.I. to generate original text. Instead, they would write everything on their own but use A.I. sparingly for auto-fill or in moments when they feel stuck.

PHASE 5
EDITING AND REVISION

As students move toward revision, they engage in a peer feedback process. A key aspect of editing and revision is asking, "how is this being received?" or "how do actual humans respond to this piece?" Most of the feedback could be the type that humans do well, such as voice, engagement, tone, and clarity.

But students could also ask for specific feedback from the chatbot. It might be something like, "How can I make my argumentation better?" or "What are some changes I could do to make the essay flow more smoothly." They might ask the A.I. to track certain data trends in their writing, like overused words or sentence length variation. Students might engage in a one-on-one writing conference with the teacher but then move back to the A.I. for additional targeted feedback.

As they shift from revising to editing, students can use a tool like Grammarly with A.I. highly tailored to improve word choice and catch mistakes.

PHASE 6
ADDING MULTIMEDIA

If students want to transform their essay, they could add a human touch by doing a video or audio essay. You can give students examples of high-quality video essays like those of the Nerdwriter1 YouTube channel.[105] Here, they combine images, video, and text with their distinctly human voice. They might sketch a few slides to illustrate key points or even animate these in the style of Common Craft videos. Students can use A.I. as a tool to generate images based on command prompts. They might also ask a chatbot to come up with ideas for images or videos to use alongside their voice.

Note that the previous example works well for persuasive and expository texts. But what does this mean when writing in other ELA genres? Here are a few ideas.

Let's consider functional / instructional texts. Students might begin by writing an initial set of steps in a how-to piece. From there, they can ask the A.I. to do the same thing. Then, comparing their own list to that of the A.I., students can add steps and perhaps even rearrange the sequence. Afterward, they can write out the directions and use the A.I. to get feedback. You might give students a prompt to use like, "Have the A.I. give you feedback on simplicity and clarity." Afterward, students might read each other's directions and attempt to do the task. They can then give feedback of how an actual human perceives the text.

What about narrative writing? Students can use generative A.I. to help develop characters, come up with plot ideas, and flesh out their setting. It can be a great starting place for writing. If you've ever used story cubes or cards, this is the same idea.

If this feels as though the A.I. is doing too much of the writing process, you can set certain parameters. You might skip A.I. in the actual text-generation portion (phase 4). You might create certain guidelines where students have to create at least 4 entirely original paragraphs.

As a teacher, you might want to introduce A.I. tools slowly with careful modeling. This blended approach requires constant critical thinking and analysis, and some students will struggle along the way. I recently worked with a high school teacher who incorporated A.I. into the writing process. Some students chose to avoid it entirely. Others used it but only after the teacher had modeled the process and students engaged in guided practice. Like any powerful tool, generative A.I. requires training and practice to use it effectively. For this reason, we will likely use it incrementally with younger students and continue to focus on human-generated writing. This is where each teacher's expertise in human development becomes critical.

RETHINKING ACCOUNTABILITY

SURVEILLANCE
AND PUNISHMENTS

TRUST
AND ACCOUNTABILITY

WHAT ABOUT ACCOUNTABILITY?

Notice that this blended approach shifts accountability away from surveillance and punishments and toward trust and transparency. Students use A.I.-generated text but it is timestamped in a shared document (like a Google Document). They then modify the A.I.-generated text with a color-coded process that makes it easy to visualize how much of the text is human-generated. In using this process, I've found that students have re-arranged paragraphs, added entirely new paragraphs, and amplified their writing far beyond the initial A.I.-generated text.

I mention this because I've already had several people reach out to me asking if I would test their A.I. detection software. These programs promise to detect cheating by analyzing a piece of writing and detecting whether it was human generated. Within a minute, you receive a score describing how much of the work has been generated by A.I. Oddly enough, these programs are a form of A.I. The complex algorithms look at a series of factors to determine if something was A.I. generated. So, we are using A.I. to catch A.I. Sounds a bit like *Blade Runner*.

The A.I.-detection programs look for patterns in our writing. Human thought tends to be more logical but also contains random digressions. In other words, we tend to take random rabbit trails. Human writers tend to have distinct styles and tones that are shaped by their experiences, personality, and background, whereas A.I.-generated writing may be more generic and lacking in personality. We also use more colloquial language, like the aforementioned rabbit trails. We tend to change verb tenses more often as well.

I've tested out nine of these programs with abysmal results. I used unpublished writing of my own, a series of student pieces (with permission), and a bunch of A.I. prompts generated by ChatGPT. I then used some pieces that contain a hybrid of both. In each case, I found that these algorithms struggled to determine the A.I.-generated prompts when they were a human-A.I. hybrid. But more alarming, there were many false positives. The A.I. kept identifying unpublished human work as A.I.-generated.

To put it in perspective, imagine a teacher with six class periods that each have 30 students. Throughout a semester, the students each submit five essays. If that teacher uses an A.I. detection software with a success rate of 94%, this will still mean that up to 54 students might be either falsely accused of cheating or getting away with cheating.

When we focus accountability on "catching cheaters," we entrust advanced algorithms to judge the academic integrity of our students. Imagine being a student who wrote something entirely from scratch only to find that you failed a class and faced academic probation because a robot sucks at determining what is human. Even as the algorithms improve in detecting A.I.-generated text, this approach leans heavily into Lock It and Block It approach.

Fortunately, there's a more human approach to accountability. It's the trust and transparency approach that my professor friend brought up when she first heard about ChatGPT. Instead of panicking and moving into a lockdown approach, she asked, "How can we have students use the tools and make their thinking visible?"

We can't predict what writing will look like in a world dominated by artificial intelligence. Generative A.I. is still in an early phase of development. Machine learning will grow more advanced and complex in the upcoming decades. Focusing on "catching cheaters" sets us up in an endless cat and mouse game that fails to build on the values of trust and student agency.

Generative A.I. is part of yet another stage in the evolution of human writing. The printing press led to a rise in literacy rates and a more formal and complex structure for writing. The advent of radio and television has corresponded with a more informal tone and structure in the written word. Likely, A.I. will transform our approach to writing in ways that we cannot predict. The key will be to retain the human element and use A.I. tools wisely.

CHAPTER 14

INTEGRATING ARTIFICIAL INTELLIGENCE INTO SCIENCE

"Mr. Spencer, you *do* know that we all have phones, right?" a student asks.

"*Most* of you," I correct him.

"If a student doesn't have a phone, they can use their Chromebooks. It's way faster and more accurate," another student says.

"That's not why we're doing this," I point out.

"I'm not an artist. I hate drawing," another student adds.

"I know this sounds strange but when you draw what you see, you become a better observer," I explain. I cringe at the collective sigh of my students.

"I'm serious. This isn't about art. This isn't about drawing. This is about learning how to observe. When you draw what you see, you pay closer attention."

My students move through each of the five stations sketching out the examples of organism adaptations. A feather here. A tooth there. A few plants. A mushroom (no, not the kind that makes you see anything magical).

I have a reason for this activity. I want students to slow down and notice the physical world. I want them to study the specimens without the aid of a screen. The act of sketching helps students learn how to see and observe.[106]

As we move into a peer discussion, students begin critiquing the realism of one another's drawings. This isn't about artistic talent. The focus is on function. What did they draw accurately? What did they capture and what did they miss? Students talk about what they saw, what they missed, and how these adaptations might help an organism thrive in its habitat.

After revising their initial sketches, they annotate their drawings. They describe their hypothesis of how natural selection might have occurred and why each organism is able to thrive in its habitat. In this moment, the learning is clear, concrete, and visible. My goal is for students to observe with intention in a world full of digital distractions. I want them to learn the art of focused observation.

START WITH HANDS-ON LEARNING

On the surface, it would seem like science class would be the best place to transform learning with A.I. The dynamic element of chatbots makes the back-and-forth inquiry process more feasible. Moreover, scientists are already using A.I. for data analysis and predictive models.[107] Why not have students can use A.I. tools to process data from experiments, simulations, or surveys? Students could then use A.I. to create predictive models to help understand complex scientific phenomena.

A high school chemistry class might use A.I. to predict the outcomes of a chemical reaction. A biology class might use A.I. to predict the spread of an infectious disease. Even an early elementary class might use A.I. to see what happens to food chains when an apex predator becomes endangered.

However, authentic science is inherently tactile. Students learn to think like scientists by using their sensory memory to make sense out of the world around them. They need to ask questions and design experiments that they do with their actual hands. In other words, hands-on learning should require their actual hands.

For this reason, as we imagine our A.I. roadmap, we want to begin with a physical, human-oriented approach to science and only augment with A.I. when it is necessary.

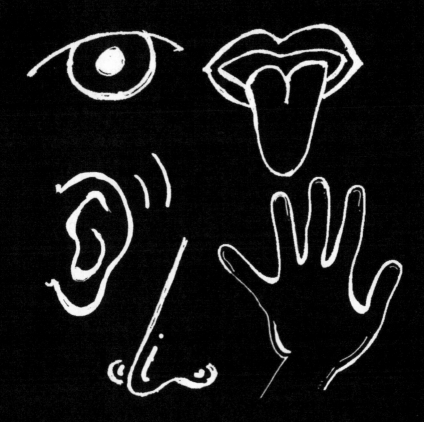

SCIENCE IS SENSORY

There's something powerful about seeing chemical reactions in real-time and observing it with your eyes or smelling the result of a reaction with your nose. This should be supervised with proper equipment following tight protocols. But a lab should be a location with manipulatives and materials. It should be a place where students learn how to think like scientists by discovering answers to their driving questions and learning to trust what they see in the material world.

There's a place for A.I. within the curriculum but authentic science should begin with the human element and only use machine learning for specific cases of augmentation. In other words, just because we *can* use A.I. in science doesn't mean we *should* use it in a science class. Still, there are some potential uses of A.I. within science that place the humanity at the forefront. In this chapter, we explore what this dynamic might look like.

STEAM PROJECTS

In the future, so many of our biggest challenges will need collaboration from the sciences and the humanities. From a young age, students can learn how to think in this connected way by engaging in STEAM (Science, Technology, Engineering, Arts, and Math) projects. STEAM projects are inherently interdisciplinary They bridge the artificial gap between the arts and the sciences in a way that represents a more rhizomatic approach to learning.

STEAM projects aim to provide students with a holistic learning experience that encourages the types of human skills A.I. can't do. With a STEAM project, students might build and design prototypes, conduct experiments, engage in coding, create science-based art installations, or solve a complex social problem using the engineering cycle. This hands-on, experiential learning provides students with a deeper understanding of the world around them. Often, students complete these projects in a makerspace.

There are many models you might use. It could be a design thinking process, a PBL process, or an inquiry-based learning process. But, in general, STEAM projects will have some of the following elements.

A.I. WITHIN MAKERSPACES

In the future, automation and A.I. will replace so many aspects of creative work. It seems counterintuitive, then, that the solution might just be found in a hands-on makerspace. By giving students access to makerspaces within STEAM projects, we can help them develop what Dale Doughtery calls the "maker mindset."[108]

A makerspace is a collaborative workspace that provides students with access to tools necessary for creating, inventing, and exploring.

Makerspaces generally offer resources such as 3D printers, laser cutters, woodworking tools, electronics equipment, and software for designing and prototyping. The goal is to foster a culture of learning, experimentation, and creativity. In a makerspace, students come together to learn new skills, work on projects, and collaborate with others. In this sense, it's not about the technology. It's about the making.

In some cases, the technology does too much of the heavy lifting. I've seen STEM classes where students take free templates from the internet and 3D print them off without making many modifications. The finished products look amazing but there was no true creative thinking involved.

By contrast, when students prototype by hand, they have a better sense of the actual physics involved in prototyping. When students make tiny tweaks to the roller coaster that they're building by hand, they get to feel it evolve and experience it in a more temporal way. When they play around with the circuitry (safely with circuitry kits), they can sense how electricity works. There's something magical about that moment in a hands-on robotics project where they get their machine to finally pick up an object. After tons of iterations, when it finally works, you'll often see students cheering.

So, what does this have to do with artificial intelligence? With automation, the A.I. can do all this creative thinking ahead of time. We can outsource significant aspects of the STEAM projects to the machines. But if the goal is to learn how to think creatively, we need students to engage in the hands-on elements of a STEAM project. In other words, the maker space is a location where we can do by hand what machines can do in a faster and more automated way. As students engage in this hands-on learning, they become divergent thinkers and problem-solvers. They learn to "do differently" what machines can do quickly.

This doesn't mean we avoid A.I. Often, students will use elements of A.I. in a mash-up with the hands-on materials. For example, they might use A.I. for research and clarification during a STEAM project. They might do a hands-on project but then run it through an A.I.-related digital modeling project. Students might do a robotics and circuitry project and use A.I. to generate some of the initial code or debug some of their own code to see what's not working.

A makerspace focuses on the human element first and incorporates A.I. when necessary. It's messy and organic.

A.I.-DRIVEN DIGITAL MODELING

The need for a physical, tactile makerspace doesn't mean we have to abandon A.I. entirely. We can use machine learning in a way that helps fill in the gaps in key areas that a physical classroom might lack.

One example is the virtual lab, which can help students explore and interact with scientific concepts in a safe and controlled environment. These labs combine artificial intelligence and virtual reality for an experience that is dynamic and adaptative:

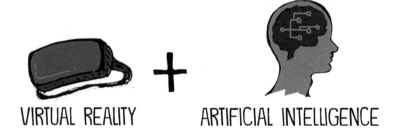

VIRTUAL REALITY   +   ARTIFICIAL INTELLIGENCE

Consider the role of dissections. These are not only expensive but also involve ethical issues for some students and their families. With machine learning, students can engage in virtual dissection labs in a way that respects their personal values.

A.I. can help model complex scientific concepts and phenomena that would otherwise be too difficult to study in a typical classroom setting. Most high school classrooms don't have the budget for an electron microscope. A basic transmission electron microscope (TEM) can cost anywhere from tens of thousands to hundreds of thousands of dollars. More sophisticated TEM models can cost well over a million dollars. That's just the beginning. Then you have ongoing costs associated with maintaining, operating, and repairing an electron microscope.

Generative A.I. can help simulate the behavior of subatomic particles. Instead of merely viewing an example via video, students can use A.I. coupled with 3D modeling to engage in a simulation that mirrors what one would experience with an electron microscope. Imagine students generating their own chemistry questions with no significant concerns for cost or safety. They could then set the parameters for a digital simulation using an interactive A.I. At some point, this might even involve virtual reality for a deeper immersive experience.

Similarly, students might use A.I.-fueled modeling to study the potential spread of diseases, the effects of climate change on the environment, or the impact of an invasive species on a local habitat. In physics, students might use digital modeling with A.I. to study fluid dynamics in a hydroelectric dam STEM project. In chemistry, an A.I. simulation might help students understand the role of covalent bonds in everyday life.

At some point, students might combine the physical, hands-on experiences of a STEM project with a predictive A.I. modeling process as they engage in the protoyping process. If they're working on a roller coaster design project to study Newton's Laws, students would play with the physical objects. They would prototype in the physical world using upcycled materials (pipes, plastic, deconstructed toy cars, duct tape) but also engage in digital modeling. Then, using generative A.I., students could convert this physical prototype into a virtual model that could eventually become a 3D roller coaster experience. The students could use a similar process to design their own transportation methods or create a more weather-proof home.

At a younger age, students might engage in this A.I.-generated virtual reality as they learn about weather systems and changes to the climate. A virtual reality simulation could allow students to explore the inside of a plant or the behavior of different animals in their natural habitats. They might get a chance to check out the inside of an animal cell.

Consider all the bizarre field trips that Ms. Frizzle took with her students (which never seemed to follow any of the required safety protocols I had to use on field trips) in *The Magic School Bus*. Many of these might become a (virtual) reality, with the A.I. adapting to student input as it generates new worlds for students to discover.

Note that the physical element should precede the digital modeling fueled by A.I. Sometimes the best option will be a hand-drawn picture of a bean just starting to sprout out of a paper of a cup or a container full of pond water that slowly turns into an entire ecosystem. Here kids ask, "Where did this life come from?" from there, they move into deeper inquiry as they learn to observe, ask, and test hypotheses.

However, we can couple these hands-on experiences with A.I.-infused digital modeling and virtual reality. We can find strategic moments where A.I. can work with digital modeling or virtual reality to offer learning experiences that would normally be far too costly for a typical K-12 classroom.

As we think about the notion of the maze, our students will need to think like scientists. They will need to ask hard questions, experiment, observe, and iterate. They will do so in a hands-on, human way. But they can also focus on the ethical use of A.I. within science to augment the learning.

CHAPTER 15
INTEGRATING ARTIFICIAL INTELLIGENCE INTO SOCIAL STUDIES

Your mind is not a computer. That's obvious, right? However, we tend to use computer metaphors to describe human cognition. It's so subtle, though, that we often miss it.

The reason can be explained by the Conceptual Metaphor Theory.[109] At any given moment, there is an implied metaphor that shapes our language. According to George Lakoff and Mark Johnson, our understanding of abstract concepts is based on our experience with more concrete concepts. You can understand how people think about abstract ideas by finding the implied metaphors.

We might use the metaphor of "time as money" when we use terms like saved, wasted, or spent. Similarly, the metaphor of "love is a journey" suggests that love is a process that can have ups and downs, twists and turns, and destinations. We know that a conversation is becoming an argument when people use war metaphors: getting heated, getting defensive, shoot down an argument, attack a weak point.

We are immersed in world of unspoken metaphors. These metaphors shape the language we use as we make sense out of reality. By examining the language, we can determine the implied metaphor. So, what does this have to do with A.I.? I'm getting there, I promise. But first, I'm going to share just a little more history because . . . well . . . I love history.

Historically, people tend to describe the mind with a metaphor of the latest technology. In ancient China, Confucius described the mind as a container. The mind was able to know the Way "by being empty, one, and quiet." Ancient Hebrews described the affective elements of thinking (the heart) as a stone tablet and a diamond stylus. To the Ancient Greeks, the mind was a malleable wax tablet. John Locke's "tabula rasa" this was a blank paper in an era dominated by the printing press. Later Enlightenment thinkers would use language related to machines, theater, and paintings.

By the late 1800's, German physicist Hermann von Helmholtz used a telegraph metaphor to describe human cognition. Half a century later, Otto Loewi used the language of the telegraph to describe his discovery of the first neurotransmitter while experimenting with frogs. Thus, the brain could "send and receive signals" to other neurons. We would then "decode" the information.

By the mid-1950's, a new metaphor emerged. Information Processing Theory used computer metaphors to describe short-term and long-term memory, relying on terms like "storage," "retrieval," "transfer" and "data" to describe the way we think. This language still dominates many conversations about information processing and Cognitive Load Theory. Currently, we are likely to see terms like "hardwired" and "processing" and "turned off."

This is partly due to the way we forge our tools as a reflection of ourselves. We use human terms to describe mechanical processes. Thus, when designing a computer, we use the term "memory" to describe its data storage capacity. Moreover, scientists, engineers, and inventors, often design tools that reflect human systems. As mentioned before, generative A.I. is modeled after neural networks that mirror human cognition. Some anthropologists even view the human mind as a form of technology. While the brain is a biological phenomenon, the mind is social, cultural, and technological.

So, here's where it matters. The mind isn't a computer and yet we use that implied metaphor all the time. If we think about something like trauma or neuroplasticity, terms like "hardwired" or "retrieval" don't capture the affective realm of thinking. In this sense, a wax tablet makes more sense (being both malleable and permanent).

Moreover, the computer metaphor within information processing misses the ebb and flow of synaptic connections and the role of neural pruning that goes on. Moreover, if we assume that learning is mechanical and can be reduced to information retrieval, we might miss the role that emotions play in helping with that retrieval process. In addition, the emerging studies on sleep and memory remind us that our brains don't exactly "recharge" in the same way that a computer does when you shut it down and restart. It's complicated and organic.

In terms of memory, we often use photography metaphors. We mention snapshots in time and talk about filters and worldviews. We talk about memories fading. But this misses the fact that memories evolve each time we access them. Remembering is an act of imagination and creativity. Memories don't simply fade. They evolve. This can have huge implications for things like eyewitness testimony in trials.

If we want to understand the human mind, we might want to make sense out of the way our technological metaphors are shaping the way we view ourselves. We might find that a wax tablet or a goblet or a garden or a lamp can help us escape the limitations of viewing the mind as a computer.

This is especially true in an era of smart machines. Generative A.I. is based on neural networks inspired by the structure and function of the human brain. This term reflects the idea of creating a computer system that can "learn" in a similar way to the human brain.

But computers can't think. They process information. Humans think. Human cognition is affective and emotional. It's unpredictable and messy. It's inherently social and relational. We use the term "intelligence" to describe A.I. But a chatbot isn't sentient. It's not affective. It will do no thinking without a prompt. When I leave the room, the chatbot is not daydreaming or making plans for the future or feeling insecure about that super awkward thing that happened yesterday. A chatbot feels no shame, has no hopes, and experiences no loss. It can generate a love poem but it can't be heartbroken. And yet, those are all major aspects of human cognition.

YOUR MIND IS NOT A COMPUTER

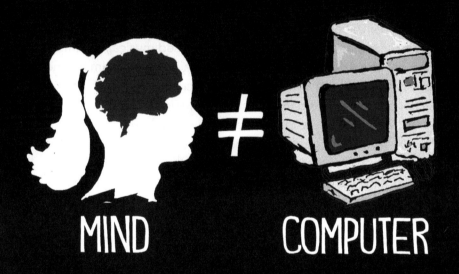

MIND ≠ COMPUTER

The mind metaphor is a small example of how history can expand our knowledge of the present. A look into the past can provide clarity for the present. In a sense, the present tense can function like an echo chamber. What seems like a broad range of perspectives might be limited by our current context. When we teach students to step back from the echo chamber of the present moment and enter a previous era, they can hear old voices that offer fresh perspectives on the present situation.

Consider the role of social media. Currently, we have seen a rise of citizen journalism. The gatekeepers are gone and now anyone can publish anything. We now live in an era of filter bubbles, where politics have grown more polarized, and the rhetoric is more intense. It's easier than ever to spread misinformation and it will continue to accelerate with the combination of deep fakes and generative A.I.

While this feels like an entirely new phenomenon, the United States experienced a similar phenomenon in the early 1800's. For all the talk of polarization, this was an era where politicians fought in duels (and later inspired an amazing hip hop infused musical). A simple glimpse into the Adams and Jefferson campaign reveals rumors and conspiracy theories that rival anything your cranky uncle just posted on Facebook. Some of Adams's opponents, suggested that he was prone to "monarchical" tendencies and may have been mentally unstable.[110] A few newspapers suggested Adams had having a "hideous hermaphroditical character, which has neither the force and firmness of a man, nor the gentleness and sensibility of a woman." Meanwhile, Adams's supporters accused Jefferson of being a secret agent for the French.

Newspapers at the time used to include large margins on the side where people could leave comments. Newspapers were passed around pubs or sent back and forth in the mail. You might imagine that the comments remained civil and sophisticated in that bygone era, but they often turned heated and ugly — not unlike the flaming comments you see in the online comment sections of your local newspaper.

When students explore this historical media landscape, they can make sense out of the pros and cons of having no real information gatekeepers. They see examples of hoaxes and fake news. They look at biased editorials with loaded language and propaganda. But they also see how the democratization of media allowed largely unpopular ideas to spread – bold ideas like women's suffrage and abolitionism that are now nearly universally accepted.

Students can also explore how major media outlets have impacted public policy. Consider the role of William Randolph Hearst and the Spanish-American War. His paper, *The New York Journal*, engaged in sensationalistic and often inaccurate reporting about events in Cuba, portraying the Spanish as brutal oppressors and inflaming public opinion against them.[111] This "yellow journalism" helped to create a war fever in the United States, with many Americans demanding intervention in Cuba.

As a teacher, you might do a larger thematic unit or project on technology and power. This could explore the rise of the nation-state after the printing press and move through the present day where changes in automation and machine learning have led to globalization and a rise of conservative movements.

But it doesn't have to be a whole project or thematic unit. You can find moments within your current units to highlight the ways technology impacted social, economic, and political systems. By exploring the past, students can then make sense out the present world of machine learning.

SOCIAL STUDIES IS A NATURAL SPACE FOR STUDENTS TO ANALYZE HOW A.I. IMPACTS OUR WORLD

Dr. John Spencer

THE POWER OF DIALOGUE

Socrates believed that writing would cause people to rely too much on the written word, rather than their own memories. He believed that people who read a text would only be able to interpret it in the way that the author intended, rather than engaging in a dialogue with the ideas presented and coming to their own conclusions. Moreover, Socrates was concerned that writing could be used to spread false ideas and opinions.

Sound familiar? These are many of the same concerns people have with A.I. While it's easy to write off Socrates as reactionary, he had a point. We lost a bit of our humanity when we embraced the printed word. And we continue to lose parts of our humanity when we give up aspects of our brains to machines. We are meant to live with our five senses.

However, I love the written word. I love getting lost in a novel or thinking hard about an idea. I love crafting together sentences and weaving together stories. I love listening to an audiobook on a long car ride. But I also love turning the radio off, listening to the silence, and enjoying the moment. I love drawing with Micah, playing pool with Joel, and dreaming up story ideas with Brenna. I love long conversations in the hot tub with Christy. I love breaking bread and telling stories with our neighbors as we sit around a firepit.

Technology dehumanizes us as it pulls us away from the natural world, but it also allows us to do the deeply human work of creative thinking. Making stuff is part of what makes us human. On some level, this has nothing to do with teaching. But on another level, it has everything to do with teaching. As educators, we can invite students into a Socratic dialogue about A.I. and how it shapes our world.

The following are some critical thinking questions we might ask secondary students to consider in a Socratic dialogue about A.I.:

- Where am I using A.I. without even thinking?
- How does A.I. actually work?
- How might people try to use A.I. to inflict harm? How might people try to use A.I. to benefit humanity? What happens when someone tries to use it for good but accidentally causes harm?
- What does A.I. do well? What does it do poorly?
- What are some things I would like A.I. to do? What is the cost in using it?
- What are some things I don't want A.I. to do? What is the cost in avoiding it?
- How am I combining A.I. with my own creative thoughts, ideas, and approaches?
- What is the danger in treating robots like humans?
- What are the potential ethical implications of A.I., and how can we ensure that A.I. is aligned with human values? What guardrails do we need to set up for A.I.?
- What are some ways that A.I. is already replacing human decision-making? What are the risks and benefits of this?
- What types of biases do you see in the A.I. that you are using?
- Who is currently benefiting and who is currently being harmed by the widespread use of A.I. and machine learning? How do we address systems of power?
- When do you consider a work your own and when do you consider it A.I.-generated? When does it seem to be doing the thinking for you and when is it simply a tool?
- What are some ways A.I. seems to work invisibly in your world? What is it powering on a regular basis?

This is simply a set of questions to start a dialogue. The goal is to spark a deeper, more dynamic conversation.

Questions will look different at a younger grade. Here are a few questions you might ask:

- What is artificial intelligence, and how does it work?
- Can you think of any examples of A.I. that you encounter in your daily life?
- What are some good and bad things about A.I.?
- Should there be rules or limits on how A.I. is used? If so, what might those rules be?
- How do you think A.I. will change the way we live and work in the future?

As a teacher, we can encourage students to explore these questions through a Socratic Seminar.

POTENTIAL USES FOR A.I. IN SOCIAL STUDIES

Social studies is a great space to help students make sense out of how A.I. is shaping their world. But we can also incorporate A.I. into the social studies classroom in certain strategic ways.

- **Generative A.I. for Conceptual Understanding:** As mentioned before, A.I. can be a great way to help students make sense out of social studies concepts. For example, if a student struggles to understand the major economic systems and philosophies, they could go to a chat bot and ask, "What is communism, capitalism, and socialism?" From there, they could ask follow-up questions like, "What is the difference between socialism and democratic socialism?" They might ask for examples and features of a mixed economy. Here, they actively engage in a question and answer with a focus on curiosity. Meanwhile, they build on their prior knowledge. There's a danger here in the bias of a chatbot, so we need to incorporate many of the previously mentioned strategies in the chapter on information literacy.
- **Leveled Skill Practice:** A.I.-powered systems can help students learn social studies skills through personalized instruction and feedback. These systems use machine learning algorithms to

adapt the content and pace of instruction to the needs of each student. A student might use it to practice a challenging discrete skill in economics (understanding price fluctuations in markets, for example). Or it might involve a set of skill practices in history, like decoding a timeline or analyzing a primary source document. A word of caution. There's a danger in isolating these skills away from a larger authentic context, so I would use this practice sparingly.

- **Embedded in PBL**: As mentioned before, students can use A.I. in every aspect of a social studies PBL. They can use generative A.I. in developing their inquiry questions and begin the research process. When texts are too complex, A.I. tools can help simplify the language or translate passages into a student's native language. They might use generative A.I. (including text-based, A.I. art, or A.I. audio) as they design their creative prototypes.

- **Natural Language Processing**: A.I.-powered natural language processing tools can help teachers assess students' writing skills, provide feedback, and identify areas where students need additional support. So, an A.I. feedback tool might help students with a complex video essay or a simpler DBQ (Document Based Question).[112]

- **Designing Social Studies Learning Centers**: At the early elementary years, you might have a hard time finding grade-appropriate resources for certain areas of social studies. Teachers can use generative A.I. to create informational texts at different reading levels and then use a combination of public domain images and A.I.-generated images to add visuals. Finally, they can design reading comprehension questions and graphic organizers that students use as they rotate from center to center. They might be learning about the daily life of ancient Roman cities with students working in teams but reading individually at their own reading level.

- **Interactive Simulations**: A.I.-powered simulations can help students explore historical events and social phenomena in an interactive and engaging way. These simulations can help students develop critical thinking skills, learn how to analyze data, and practice decision-making.

Let's take a deeper dive into this last idea of simulations.

GAME-BASED SIMULATIONS

Picture this. I'm in the third grade and it's my turn at the Apple II. My friend Mike R. is shaking his head. "We're doomed. I'm telling you, we're doomed. Anything we try won't work. Everyone just gets dysentery."

Mike L. scoots his chair back. "It's rigged. Everyone gets dysentery. It's a dysentery game. They shouldn't even call it Oregon Trail. Just call it Dysentery."

The prompt pops up and we deliberate. We're somewhere between the west and the Midwest and I am determined to make it to Oregon. We click on the option and trudge forward. A new prompt pops up.

"Bam! No dysentery," I point out.

"Not yet," Mike P. says as he walks by. If it seems like we had a lot of Mikes, let me remind you that the year was 1989. Mike was the Aiden of the 1980s.

We continue with a new game prompt, and I start to feel hopeful. True, there's snow on the ground but I'm thinking we might just make it. We handle a broken wagon wheel. We keep warm with enough clothes. But then . . . a hunting accident. Is that really an option? We did everything right! I'm enraged.

Looking back on this game, it feels so primitive. The green pixilated graphics. The multiple choice prompts. The lack of dynamic characters. And yet, this was an early example of A.I. for simulations. If you didn't grow up in the U.S. in the 1980s, the Oregon Trail was a wildly popular computer game that simulated the experience of traveling westward by covered wagon in the 19th century. The game was first created in 1971 by a group of student teachers at Carleton

College in Northfield, Minnesota, and has since been revised and updated several times.[113]

Players took on the role of a pioneer family or group traveling from Missouri to Oregon in 1848. The goal was to make it to Oregon while facing challenges, such as bad weather, sickness, lack of food and water, and, of course, dysentery. This simulation focused on making decisions about how to allocate resources such as food and money.

While we didn't think of it as A.I., the Oregon Trail used algorithms to simulate the various events and challenges that pioneers encountered on their westward journey. The algorithms determined the likelihood of encountering certain events (such as bad weather, illness, or bandit attacks), the rate at which resources like food and water are consumed, and the impact of player decisions on the outcome of the game. For me, the Oregon Trail made history come alive. As silly as it may sound, I identified with that pioneer family.

There have been some critiques of the Oregon Trail. Students never asked about the Native America perspective, or the power dynamics involved in "settling" a new land. Nostalgia aside, I recognize that I learned a very one-sided view of U.S. history.

As we think about using simulations in social studies, we need to recognize the need for multiple perspectives and multiple narrative strands. We should pay careful attention to the role of bias within the simulation. We want to avoid any simulation that might involve trivializing injustice or trauma.[114] For example, we should avoid a slave escape game or a game that simulates being in the Holocaust.

There's also the danger of oversimplification. Simulations necessarily simplify complex historical events and issues to make them more accessible to students. However, this simplification can sometimes lead to an inaccurate or incomplete portrayal of the past, which can be misleading or even harmful if students come away with an oversimplified understanding of a complex topic.

Similarly, simulations can lack deeper context, making it hard for students to understand how the events fit into the broader historical narrative. Students end up with a fragmented understanding of history. For this reason, simulations should include a concept attainment lesson ahead of time so students can see the context of the simulation. You might also need to create opportunities for students to read some primary and secondary sources to help students see the human element of history. This is why it's critical that students engage in reflection during and after a simulation.

Despite these challenges, A.I.-informed simulations can be an immersive way for students to learn social studies. Simulations can increase student engagement and focus. When done well, a simulation can humanize history, geography, or economics. Simulations can also help students develop empathy by requiring them to take on the roles of people with different backgrounds and experiences. Often, they learn history at a deeper level with multiple perspectives.

Generative A.I. can make simulations more adaptive and realistic. Unlike the multiple-choice options of the Oregon Trail game, new simulations will ask students to think creatively as they interact with multiple characters. Some characters might be classmates, but others may be non-player characters (NPCs) who seem to act in a more human way than the typical NPC stereotype. In other words, generative A.I. makes the NPC more dynamic and human.

Imagine being in a high school economics class. You've thought about college and trade school. You've seen the numbers on student loan debt. Your teacher talked about investment portfolios, but it didn't stick. You heard your parents talking about a 15-year versus 30-year mortgage and you have no idea what words like APR mean. You'll leave high school in 3 months, but all of this feels like a foreign world. It's scary but also . . . distant.

Now imagine doing a simulation. It goes beyond the typical stock market simulation. This is a life simulation. Each day covers another year in your life. You must adapt to new challenges. You make decisions about college and career. You face an economic downturn that nobody expected. You place money in stocks and watch those numbers go up and down. You practice budgeting but also learn about the downsides of budgeting when it treats money as non-fungible. You engage in discussions and debates with classmates. Suddenly, this all seems real. It's sometimes too fast. But then again, sometimes life can feel too fast as well.

Through this simulation, you learn about money markets, stocks, supply and demand, and macroeconomics. You see how monetary policies impact daily life. You learn about personal finance, including debt, investments, and budgeting. You learn some quirky ideas from behavioral economics about the irrational ways that we think about money. As you interact with others, you gain empathy and see new perspectives.

Now imagine you are a fourth grader. You're also learning about economics but this time it's far simpler. Think supply and demand. Some basic of budgeting. You get the idea. You show up to school and learn that you'll be designing a virtual store. Classmates and fictional characters interact with you as you do market research and design your business. You do some basic math at your grade level. You engage in problem-solving and systems thinking. You get a cartoon avatar and a make-believe currency. But you, too, get a chance to engage in collaborative problem-solving and creativity.

If we think about A.I. in social studies, we want to use it in a way that retains the human element. We need students to explore previous ideas of the past and engage in deep dialogue about A.I. and how it's shaping our world. But as we integrate A.I. into the learning, students should gain empathy and see multiple perspectives.

Dr. John Spencer

CHAPTER 16
INTEGRATING
ARTIFICIAL INTELLIGENCE
INTO THE ARTS

In a world of A.I., we will need engineers who can solve complex problems, but we'll also need artists to push our thinking and remind us of our humanity. We'll need artists who can pose the hard questions that the algorithm doesn't generate. We'll need science, yes, but also science fiction, to expand our thinking and force us to reckon with a world of smart machines.

When students learn to think like artists, they learn to think divergently. Art encourages students to think outside the box by rethinking the box. Here they come up with unique ideas and innovative solutions. Students learn to communicate big ideas and offer a new perspective with nuance. They learn how to pose hard questions to the world. When working collaboratively, students learn how to communicate with others and solve problems together as they work toward a common goal.

On some level, as we think about the future of the arts in a world of A.I., we need to recognize that much of it will remain the same. Students will need to sketch and paint. They'll need to sculpt with their hands. They'll need to memorize lines and perform in theater. They'll need to sing in a choir and feel the power of the collective human voice. They'll need to learn the violin through trial and error. They might even need to continue to work their way through "Hot Cross Buns" on the recorder. Much respect to my elementary music teacher friends who joyfully move through the "Hot Cross Buns" recorder unit every year.

And yet, while we want to keep the arts human-centered, there are some significant opportunities for using A.I. within the creative process.

Dr. John Spencer

A.I. AND THE ART CLASS

In September of 2022, artist Jason Allen won the first-place prize based in the Colorado State Fair art competition with a work he created using Midjourney, an A.I. text-to-image art generator. Many artists claimed that this wasn't true art; that Allen had merely copied and pasted the work of a machine.[115]

Around the same time, artist Greg Rutkowski noticed a disturbing trend. Rutkowski is a digital artist who creates stunning works of fantasy. But within a few weeks of Stable Diffusion's launch, he noticed that so much of the digital art seemed to mirror his unique style.[116]

"It's been just a month. What about in a year? I probably won't be able to find my work out there because it will be flooded with A.I. art," Rutkowski pointed out.

A.I.-generated art is having a moment right now. We see it commercially in blog posts and magazine articles. We see it with stylized profile pictures. To some, this is the death of art. To others, it's the latest iteration of the craft.

A.I. image generators run on machine learning. The process usually begins with a dataset of images that the A.I. model processes. The model then uses this data to create its own unique output based on the patterns it has identified in the dataset. Another approach is to use "neural style transfer," which involves taking a content image (perhaps a photo of a peanut butter and jelly sandwich) and applying the style of another image (such as a surrealist painting) to it. This is done by training an A.I. model to recognize the content and style of images separately, and then using that knowledge to apply the style to the content image.

Many artists view this as cheating. But it's a little more complicated. After all, Dada artists pushed the limits on defining how "generative" art needed to be. Marcel Duchamp famously placed a porcelain urinal on a pedestal and signed it R. Mutt. My initial impulse is to say, "That's not really art" but that's the point of Dada. What about a mash-up of multiple media to create something new? What about the integration of technology into art?

Critics of photography once claimed it wasn't art. A photograph was too mechanical to be "real" art. Early digital art faced the same accusations. More recently, sculptors who use 3D printers have been accused of taking a shortcut that bypasses "real" sculpting.

Moreover, it's not uncommon for well-known artists to outsource aspects of their artistic process. They might use technology or automation as an editing tool. Or they might use technology to generate templates or molds that they then customize. But in some cases, artists use teams of subcontractors to execute their vision. Jeff Koons once employed over a hundred artists for his hand-painted "Gazing Ball" series.[117] Damien Hirst employed a team of artists to execute his vision of 14 massive bronze sculptures depicting various stages of pregnancy.[118] What is the creative difference between an artist training an A.I. to execute a specific brief in her style and an artist hiring other artists to execute her vision of a sculpture?

In the previous chapter on creativity, we posed the question about copyright and creativity. When A.I. uses vast amount of data, is it merely seeking inspiration from culture (something most artists do) or is it sampling copyrighted works without attribution? Is it more like a visit to a museum for inspiration or is it closer to sampling a musical artist's work in a new song?

The next decade will involve big questions about the definition of creativity, authenticity, and art itself. Art teachers can help students explore these big ideas through conversations about the meaning of art. While many art teachers will choose to avoid A.I.-generated art, some teachers might ask students to use these tools to experiment and rethink the definition of art.

Here are a few ways art teachers might use A.I. in the classroom:

- **Generating new ideas:** A.I.-generated art can be used as a source of inspiration for students, providing them with new ideas and creative possibilities. This isn't all that different from the way students currently look at art books, examples, or pages of Google Images.
- **Digital modeling:** Students might use A.I. tools for digital modeling to focus on added realism for paintings or sketches.

They could potentially generate images that they then maneuver around in a 3D space.

- **Providing students with new tools and techniques:** A.I. can be used to create new tools and software that students can use to experiment with different techniques and approaches. In other words, a student might ask, "What does expressionism look like? Give me an example with cats."
- **Guiding reflection**: Many A.I. image generators allow people to submit their own drawings. With this approach, a student might submit a sketch of their own and then receive four or five new images in different styles. The goal here wouldn't be on replacing the original drawing but on gaining a new perspective as they consider new iterations on their work.
- **Making A.I.-generated art:** Students could start out making A.I. generated art based on their own command prompts. From there, they create mash-ups of multiple styles. Or they digitally alter an A.I. image using editing software like Photoshop.

Students might pull together multiple A.I.-generated works into a single piece and then add their own unique twist. Here, it functions like a mosaic or a collage. Other times, students might take A.I.-generated work and modify it digitally with tools like Photoshop, only to reinterpret it again using A.I., before making their own modifications again. Ultimately, art class is about more than merely learning a new technique. It's about finding your voice, expressing your creativity, and making a statement to the world. A.I. might just be another tool artists use for their creative process.

GENERATING
NEW IDEAS

HELPING
WITH
REFLECTION

NEW TOOLS
AND TECHNIQUES

HELP WITH
EDITING

GENERATING
EXAMPLES
FOR INSPIRATION

HOW MIGHT ARTISTS USE A.I.?

HELPING
WITH
MARKETING

MAKING
CREATIVE WORK
FASTER

AI-GENERATED SOURCE
MATERIAL
FOR MASH-UPS

ACCESSIBILITY
FEATURES

DIGITAL MODELING

GETTING FEEDBACK

A.I. IN THE PERFORMING ARTS

When a student performs a line in a theater production, it's not merely a line. It's the culmination of hours of hard work. It's a team learning to read one another's body language, listen to critical feedback, and refine their work. It's a community of actors, set designers, and technicians working toward a common goal. It's the moment of courage when one stands in front of an audience and belts out a tune.

When a student performs in a marching band, it's not merely a line of notes. It's a community working through iterations in songs until they get it right. When a student sings in a choir, it's a collective voice that's far more powerful than what anyone could do on their own.

So, when we think about the performing arts, it's important that we start with the human element and only use A.I. as a way that can enhance the learning process. The performing arts will always be tied to the present moment. However, there are still some ways that teachers might incorporate A.I. into the performing arts.

- **Creating digital set designs:** A.I. can be used to create digital set designs and 3D models of the set, which can be used to visualize the set and make changes before the physical set is built. This can save time and resources and allow for more experimentation with different designs.
- **Virtual rehearsals:** A.I. can be used to create virtual rehearsals, allowing actors to rehearse with virtual characters and sets. This can help actors to better visualize their performances and make adjustments before the rehearsals begin.
- **Voice and speech recognition:** A.I. can be used to analyze actors' voices and speech patterns, providing feedback on their performance. In music, students can use A.I. to gauge their accuracy in hitting notes.
- **Lighting and sound effects:** A.I. can be used to create and control lighting and sound effects during the performance, allowing for more precise and complex effects to be created.

- **Costume design:** A.I. can be used to create virtual costumes, allowing designers to experiment with different fabrics, colors, and patterns.
- **Performance analysis:** A.I. can be used to analyze actors' performances, providing feedback on their movements, voice, and facial expressions, and suggesting ways to improve their performance. A.I.-powered software can analyze a student's voice and provide real-time feedback on pitch, tone, and other aspects of their singing.
- **Accompaniment:** A.I. can be used to create accompaniment tracks for choir rehearsals, allowing students to practice their parts with an accompaniment even if a live accompanist is not available.

In each of these cases, A.I. can function as a tool that artists use throughout the performing arts. There may come a time when music and drama teachers blend together A.I. and live performance elements (not unlike the way certain music programs might also include music videos). But it's important that remember the power of the moment. The performing arts will continue to stand apart in a world of machine learning because they are live and deeply human.

IN A WORLD OF
SMART MACHINES,
WE NEED THE ARTS
TO HELP US RETAIN
OUR HUMANITY

REMEMBERING THE HUMAN ELEMENT

Generative A.I. uses neural networks to produce original artwork. However, as I've played around with it, I noticed that A.I. artwork had its own distinct style. Even when creating impressionist, mid-century modern, or street art styles, there is a certain A.I. footprint that remains.

This is why I'll continue to create my own sketches. They fit my style and capture my voice. Generative A.I. can create visuals that are better than my sketches. I get that. But I don't want better. I want my sketches. I want to take the vanilla and craft my own flavor.

But also, on a deeper level, I don't ever want to outsource this creative process to a machine. I make art because I love making art and that's not something I ever want to hand over to a machine.

As we think about the changing landscape of art in a world of A.I., we need to ensure that students find their voice and maintain their own style. Their unique fingerprint will ultimately be what sets them apart in a world of smart machines.

CHAPTER 17

INTEGRATING
ARTIFICIAL INTELLIGENCE
INTO HEALTH AND P.E.

"I think we're doing health class all wrong," a pre-service teacher tells me.

"What do you mean?" I ask.

"Okay, maybe not all wrong. But we have this curriculum that focuses on mental, physical, and social health. It's the same thing I grew up with. It's the same thing my parents grew up with. It's not bad but it's . . . incomplete."

"What needs to change?" I ask her.

"This health triangle is still relevant, but it doesn't look the same as it did a decade ago. For one, we don't have one specific self. We have multiple selves. We have online identities that exist in layers. Maybe we need a health onion? I think we all end up code switching back and forth. That's why Be Real is so popular right now. It's the rare social media app focused on being yourself in a non-curated way. But it's also just another identity. SnapChat you isn't Instagram you and Instagram you isn't Be Real you and none of that is as squeaky clean as the you that you portray for your grandparents on Facebook. My point is if we take that traditional triangle, every part of this triangle is now curated and quantified. It's less like a triangle and more like a kaleidoscope."

She then describes the role of social media in the physical realm – from the apps used to track movements, workouts, and calories to the role of social media in setting unreasonable expectations around physical health. She talks about the social element of the health triangle and the role of social media in the fear of missing out. Then she talked about social and emotional health and the pros and cons of algorithms.

Finally, she says, "What I want to know is this: can algorithms make you healthier? Can they make you happier? Can they make you more well-rounded and well-adjusted? Or should we treat algorithms as a public health crisis? Should we ban smart phone usage until a student reaches adulthood? Or is that just moral panic?" She poses a vital question for both health and PE: What are the health implications of A.I.?

Previously I mentioned Neil Postman, who posited that childhood, as a distinct stage of life, was disappearing. He contended that the line between childhood and adulthood has become blurred due to the impact of media and technology.[119]

Postman argued that the rise of electronic media, especially television, has eroded the boundaries between childhood and adulthood, as children are now exposed to the same content as adults. To be clear, this wasn't ideologically conservative or liberal. It was about being developmentally appropriate.

While Postman didn't live to see the era of smart phones and algorithms, his critique is still relevant today. What does it mean for a 12-year-old to use a device and a series of apps aimed at adults? In what ways have the distinctions between childhood and adulthood been eroded by our technology? And what does that mean as we shift toward more advanced forms of A.I.? Health teachers might be the ones who can help make sense out of these questions.

THE NEED FOR SELF-AWARENESS

Self-awareness is a critical aspect of health class. Students learn how to set goals, engage in healthy habits, and make informed decisions about their lifestyle. In a health class, students learn about exercise, healthy eating habits, stress management, and disease prevention. The goal goes beyond mastering content standards. At its core, the true goal of a Health class is to live better.

If our students are going to be self-aware in an age of A.I., then health class might be the best place for students to think critically about A.I. and how it's impacting their health. The following are a few questions you might use as you integrate this into your curriculum:

Social Health:
- How is social media impacting the way friends form and interact with one another?
- How has social media changed relationships in positive and negative ways?
- In an era of deepfakes and catfishing how will you find authenticity in online relationships?
- What boundaries do you want to create between yourself and algorithms in your social interactions?
- What role do numbers and metrics play in how we define our social connectedness?
- So many apps are designed to grab our attention. What is the cost of this? What are the benefits of connecting with others?
- Is social media largely isolating or is it helping us make meaningful connections?
- How can schools and other institutions address the role of cyberbullying?

Physical Health:
- What are the ways you track your physical health?
- Are technologies like wearable devices giving us more accurate data? What do we choose to do with this data?
- How can we leverage the role A.I. to make better physical health decisions? (Example: reminders, nudges, badges). Is there a cost in using these apps for motivational purposes?
- What are the metrics you might want to pay attention to? What are the metrics you might need to ignore?
- How are algorithms defining physical health? What is the cost of this?
- How are our devices and the gamified way in which they draw our attention impacting physical health? For example, how are they impacting our sleep cycles? How are they helping us track positive decision-making?

Mental Health:
- Wat do you feel when you scroll?

- What is the danger of the "fear of missing out?"
- How have social media apps allowed members of marginalized groups connected socially with one another?
- Does social media make us feel more alone or less alone?
- Are our algorithms making us addicted to our devices?
- How have algorithms impacted your worldview? Where do you get your view of the larger issues in the world? What are the pros and cons of this?

Notice that this is merely a starting place. You might want to solicit questions from your students. From there, you can create project-based learning units. Students might look at data, do surveys, or interview experts. You might even take it to a deeper level by design service-learning experiences that encourage students to reflect on who they are as people in doing face-to-face service and in using algorithm-based tools.

If we're going to engage in authentic learning in an era of artificial intelligence, health class is a great starting place for exploring what it means to be your authentic self.

While the previous questions center on middle school and high school health classes, teachers can have some of these conversations at the elementary level as well. In the social realm, it might involve setting limits for screen time, avoiding giving away private information, and being cognizant of how apps manipulate users. They might discuss these themes in fictional read-alouds or in simpler non-fiction texts.

A.I. FOR GOAL SETTING AND TRACKING

While it's important for students to think critically about A.I., we can also encourage students to consider ways to use A.I. as a tool for developing healthy habits. Students might use generative A.I. for goal setting and tracking. Often, a larger goal can feel too big and distant. Students grow discouraged. But instead of giving up, students can use chatbots to break the goal down into reasonable tasks and sub-tasks. What emerges is more like a plan with an opportunity to chart progress. Next, they can use A.I. might to set reminders. In trying to develop healthy habits, students might use apps powered by A.I. to track their progress toward habit mastery.

Another option relates to health monitoring. Students might use wearable devices and mobile apps that use A.I. can provide students with real-time feedback on their health status. This could then help them make informed decisions about their actions. Students might use fitness trackers to monitor their activity levels and set personalized fitness goals.

At the same time, health teachers can help students see the drawbacks of these health monitoring apps. In some cases, the use of health monitoring devices might increase anxiety relating to data and activity levels. When coupled with negative cultural messages about body image, there's the potential risk of using these devices to achieve unhealthy goals. While the research on this is still emerging, health teachers should be cognizant of the potential dangers related to wearable technology and eating disorders. For these reasons, teachers should avoid any projects or assignments that require the use of health monitoring apps. Instead, they can use these examples as a conversation starter about the pros and cons of using wearables for health monitoring.

Dr. John Spencer

CAN A.I. ACTUALLY MAKE US HEALTHIER?

USING PREDICTIVE A.I. FOR SIMULATIONS

Students might someday engage in simulations fueled by A.I. Many health classes include standards relating to disaster preparedness. While it's important that students learn the content, it's more important that they apply these lessons to their lives. A simulation relating what to do in a fire, flood, or earthquake, can make the situations seem more relevant. A.I. can be used to simulate different disaster scenarios and test the effectiveness of different individualized emergency response plans. If students do this in teams, this type of simulation can improve their ability to respond in a coordinated way.

It's important that these simulations are trauma-informed and sensitive to each student's past experiences. But an adaptive simulation can help students to add authenticity to the activity.

USING A.I. TO PROMOTE MENTAL HEALTH

In the upcoming decade, we are likely to see students using interactive A.I. and chatbots in a way that promotes mental health. This isn't the same thing as a certified counselor.[120] It's more like an emotional support A.I. Prosocial chatbots will be programmed to provide emotional support to people who are experiencing mental health challenges. These chatbots will use natural language processing to understand the user's concerns and offer empathy and encouragement.

In other cases, A.I. might be used to help monitor emotions. By analyzing the language used in conversations with the chatbot, A.I. models will detect patterns and provide insights into how the person is feeling. This could help people to identify when they are experiencing particularly difficult periods and prompt them to seek additional help.

Or the A.I. might simply provide interactive health education. Chatbots could be used to provide education about mental health issues, including symptoms, treatment options, and coping strategies. This might help to reduce the stigma associated with mental illness and increase understanding among the general population. Certain studies have found that many people like interacting with what they view as a non-judgmental robot.

Dr. Alec Couros describes our collective uneasiness this way, "Students need to be cared for. We can enhance that. We can do the things that we're doing to provide care for our students. We know that A.I. has potentially created negative psychological effects, but this could have the potential to help mitigate that."[121]

As an educator, I have mixed feelings about this. I want to believe that human interaction is the key to better mental health. There's something unnerving about using A.I. to help with mental health. And yet, I recognize that this is merely my own discomfort with an emerging technology. I like my robots to be cool and rational and unemotional. This is feels different. Then again, I love the movie *Big Hero 6* and wouldn't mind having a Baymax at my disposal.

Dr. Couros explains, "A.I. has the potential for students to be heard and understood and known. It seems odd right now but in 10 years, it's not going to feel odd anymore to use A.I. for these social and emotional reasons; to offload or replace the human connection but to augment student care."

There are significant challenges in trying to design pro-social A.I. As mentioned before, if a data set is biased (and it often is) the A.I. can perpetuate sexism and racism. However, there's also the larger question of whose values we follow in deciding what is and is not pro-social. If students end up interacting with a chatbot, what happens when the messages don't align with a family's personal values? What happens when it veers into questions of moral philosophy?

To design pro-social A.I., it is essential to understand human needs, values, and perspectives. However, A.I. developers often lack expertise in areas such as ethics, psychology, sociology, and the humanities – which can make it challenging to design A.I. that aligns with human values. As chatbots begin to act more human-like, we must ask, "What kind of human are they acting like?" When a seven-year-old interacts with a chatbot, what kind of social learning is occurring? What is that child learning from the machine?

PE AND A.I.

While most of this chapter has focused on A.I. and the health class, I want to share a few ideas of how we might use A.I. in the PE class as well:

- **Goal Setting**: Students might use A.I. to generate specific goals for PE-related activities. It might be speed in running or the ability to master a jump shot. But it might also involve things like a goal for the number of days in a row doing exercise.

- **Customized Plan:** A.I. can analyze students' fitness levels and goals and create personalized fitness plans that are tailored to their individual needs. This can help students achieve their fitness goals in a way that's more personalized and approachable. If the A.I. uses elements of motivation (badges and gamification) it could help students stay more motivated. In something like a weight training class, advanced A.I. systems might eventually reach a level where they can design plans that reduce injury while also leading to better results.

- **Targeted Skill Practice:** Often, a PE teacher will model a particular skill for the entire group. Students then practice this together while the teacher gives quick, one-on-one instruction. But an A.I.-informed process would involve a more personalized set of videos that could match each student's skill level with the instructions. This isn't a reality yet but it might emerge as a tool for differentiation in a PE class.

- **Performance Feedback:** When combined with video analysis, A.I. could provide real-time feedback to students during exercises. This could help with proper form or technique and thus reduce the likelihood of injury. But it could also be a way to learn the fundamentals of a sport, like how to kick a soccer ball or do a bump-set-spike in volleyball. In this sense, the A.I. functions like a virtual coach. It won't be as effective as a human coach, but the A.I. could potentially give more frequent feedback.

- **Choosing Teams**: Teachers might create a set of criteria for their groups. Certain students can't work well with others. Certain students seem to be more skilled. You get the idea. But then, after setting this criterion, the A.I. could help select teams in a way that's more equitable than the old school choosing kids from a line. The goal would be to create teams with similar skill levels. So, in a third-grade basketball unit, you might have three different levels of teams and each level having generally well-matched students, in terms of skill levels.

There have always been bold promises for using technology in the PE class. It's important to remember that the technology should never drive PE instruction. It should always be about promoting the physical, mental, social, and emotional development of students. Like health class, the PE class should always remain human-centered, and the A.I. should aid in making the content more relevant and authentic.

CHAPTER 18
INTEGRATING ARTIFICIAL INTELLIGENCE INTO WORLD LANGUAGES

"When will we ever use French?" a freshman complains as he walks into class.

Another student points out, "If you ever go to France, I hear they hate when people speak English. So, it's one of the few places where you actually have to learn it to visit."

"Dude, I don't ever plan to go to France," the first student shoots back. "If I did, I'd just use a translation app every time I had to say something."

It is less than 5 minutes into the first class of the new year and Rebecca[122] already faces a wall of resistance. Why world languages? Why would it matter? When would they ever use French?

In the past, she had provided brain research on the value of learning a new language. She tried to lead a class discussion on the need to reach out cross-culturally. But it never really clicked. A few students really wanted to be there, but most of her students took the class out to check a box on their graduation requirements.

This year, she starts with a story. It's a video from a refugee family from Congo. They tell their story in French and the students read it with English subtitles. Tears stream across a student's face as she watches a mom describe the challenge of navigating a library for the first time. Suddenly, "Where is the library?" doesn't feel like an irrelevant sentence from French I. Instead, it's a critical moment in someone's story.

"What are your thoughts?" the teacher asks.

Students share their connections to the story. A few bold ELL students talk about how scary it was for them to learn English as native Spanish speakers. Rebecca then asks, "Is there anything we can do?"

From here, she moves into a design thinking project. The year before, Rebecca heard about how PBL expert Trevor Muir had led his students through a service-learning project that involved making videos for refugees in their community. Inspired by this idea, she reached out to a refugee agency and students began making videos in French I and French II. They often started the videos with "I'm sorry my French isn't great. I'm going to tell you how to . . ."

Students practiced the standard vocabulary: objects in a house (and local customs in American homes), going to the grocery store, navigating public transportation, vocabulary about school. They did plenty of skill practice. But they also filmed and edited their short instructional videos. A refugee agency then added the videos to old iPod Touches and gave them to families, along with handouts and directions.

The goal was to "design with" rather than "design for." Students met with agency leaders and members of the refugee community. A few students were members of this refugee community who worked as liaisons to ensure that students were being respectful of cultural customs and norms.

At one point, a mother of three young children said, "My favorite part of the video was when he apologized for his French. I feel like I am always apologizing for my English. That felt special to me."

In a world of machine learning, our students will need to retain this human connection. They need to develop empathy. This project-based learning experience helped students develop these vital human skills.

Before we get into the idea of integrating A.I. in world languages, it's important that we recognize that world language programs of the future will need to be more than just adaptive learning programs. They will need to include authentic projects like this that connect students with a real community context. At the same time, learning another language often requires skill practice and A.I. can help as students engage in this type of practice.

WORLD LANGUAGE COURSES AREN'T MERELY ABOUT LEARNING A LANGUAGE. IT'S ALSO ABOUT LEARNING EMPATHY

USING A.I. FOR ADAPTIVE LEARNING

Have you ever been "in the zone?" Maybe you're painting or playing a sport or jamming out with friends and time seems to both slow down and speed up? You're fully present in the moment but suddenly hours go by. This is what Hungarian researcher Mihaly Csikszentmihalyi refers to as Flow Theory. He describes it this way, "The flow experience is when a person is completely involved in what he or she is doing, when the concentration is very high, when the person knows moment by moment what the next steps should be . . ."[123]

One of the key ideas in Flow Theory is that the skill level should match the challenge of a learning task. In 1987, Massimini, Csíkszentmihályi and Carli published the following 8-channel model of flow in *Finding Flow: The Psychology of Student Engagement in Everyday Life*.[124] If a task is too easy, you might experience apathy or boredom but if a task seems too hard, you'll be anxious.

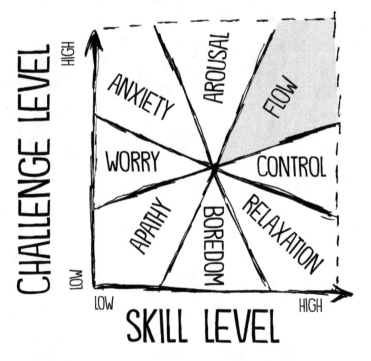

If you've ever played a video game, you've noticed this same phenomenon. The challenge is often just slightly above your skill level. You have near misses as you inch closer and closer to success. With multiple chances (think of the "lives" in Super Mario Brothers), each mistake takes you closer to success. Then, after you succeed, there's a celebration and you move up a level.

Unfortunately, we can't always structure our lessons this way as educators. We don't always have the assessment data to determine where each student is in their language learning. When we do have this data, we can't always design individualized lessons for each student. There's simply not enough time in the day to plan this. Here's where A.I. can be helpful.

Earlier, we explored the distinction between personalized learning and adaptive learning. In a human-centered approach, we often choose personalized learning over algorithm-driven adaptive learning programs. However, there's a place for adaptive learning in world language class. Adaptive learning programs walk students through language in a systematic way. As they practice the language, the A.I. adjusts the challenge of the task to meet their skill level. Certain adaptive learning programs can feel like playing a video game – with small celebrations, badges, and words of encouragement from the A.I.

As students play, they practice pronouncing words and using sentences. They watch mini-lessons showing how to conjugate verbs and they use flashcards to match words with visuals. This adaptive learning program focuses on the need for repetition, targeted instruction, and instant feedback as you practice learning a new language.

If you teach a world language, you might use an adaptive learning program for skill centers. Instead of filling out worksheets or doing sentence completion exercises, students use a program that provides instant feedback. Each student can work at their own pace and the program adapts to their current level. Adaptive learning programs focus on mastery. Mistakes are not only allowed but expected.

Sometimes, skill practice is more advanced for students. In the beginning, an adaptive learning program can work as a highly engaging way to learn vocabulary, syntax, and the foundations of a language's grammar. But over time, as students acquire more language, they will need something more advanced. Here's where generative A.I. becomes even more helpful. Here are a few ideas:

- **A.I. for Conversations:** Students interact verbally with a generative A.I. bot. The A.I. can adjust the language complexity based on how well students understand and speak the language back. At the end, each student receives feedback regarding their common mistakes.
- **A.I. for Language Clarification:** Students use an A.I. chatbot to engage in a back-and-forth conversation where they ask questions and gain a deeper understanding in that language. As they face new words that they don't understand, students ask for definitions or even translations. For certain words that have a rich contextual definition (think of the difference between *ser* and *conocer* in Spanish) the A.I. can provide clarification.
- **A.I. for Pronunciation Feedback:** The A.I. could provides specific feedback on pronunciation. As voice recognition and generative audio increase, we will likely see a proliferation of audio conversation tools that focus on this type of language practice.
- **A.I. for Written Feedback:** If a student reads a text in a world language course and writes an essay in response, the A.I. can provide feedback focusing on language acquisition.
- **A.I. for Leveled Reading:** If a world language teacher has a high interest article they are reading in another language, they can use generative A.I. to create multiple levels of the same text that students then use in a whole class discussion.
- **A.I. for Language Supports:** This might involve designing a cloze or making sentence stems or it might include finding academic vocabulary in a world language text.

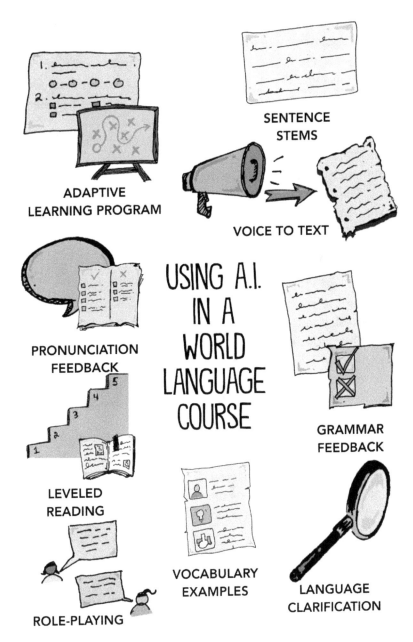

ADAPTIVE
LEARNING PROGRAM

SENTENCE
STEMS

VOICE TO TEXT

PRONUNCIATION
FEEDBACK

USING A.I.
IN A
WORLD
LANGUAGE
COURSE

GRAMMAR
FEEDBACK

LEVELED
READING

VOCABULARY
EXAMPLES

LANGUAGE
CLARIFICATION

ROLE-PLAYING

These strategies work best when having students engage in skill practice. But there's so much more to world languages. Students need to learn about cultures from around the world. They need opportunities to hear the music and eat the food. They need to know about the holidays and the stories. They need opportunities to meet people and see both the cultural differences and the shared humanity.

By using A.I. for skill practice and feedback, teachers can focus on these cultural elements. They can also incorporate elements of personalized learning through things like projects, design sprints, or discussions. This can help us remember to retain the human connection in learning a new language.

USING A.I. AS A TRANSLATOR

I step outside of my hotel and take in a breath of fresh air. It smells different here. Maybe the flora or fauna? I close my eyes and take in the sounds. The birds are different in South America. Of course, they are! But somehow it catches me off guard when I listen. I slip my phone into my pocket and head through the maze of narrow streets. I meander for the next twenty minutes, experiencing the Brazilian city with all five senses. Eventually, I find the mall.

Once there, I pull out my device. My Portuguese is rusty after two decades of neglect. The few times I attempt to speak the language, I end up slipping into Spanish instead. Fortunately, things are easier now compared to 2001. This minicomputer at the palm of my hands means I don't have to walk up to a stranger and awkwardly ask where I might find a coffee shop. I have Google Maps. When I need to read a sign, I switch to Google Translator and hold the camera up. It instantly translates the text into English with A.I.-generated augmented reality.

I pull out the translation app and type out a sentence in English and rehearse it repeatedly. Then I step into a store and explain to the clerk that I am looking for a power adapter that can handle the U.S. three-prong cord. When he answers, I use a voice-to-text translator to translate in real-time. He pulls his phone out and does the same with English. Eventually, we stop looking at each other. We just show each other our phones.

This whole process is more convenient than it was when I visited two decades ago. I can see where this might be a lifeline to someone who is navigating a new culture and new language for the first time.

And yet, I wonder what I lose in going to A.I. for language help. I think about all those awkward conversations a few decades ago, where I attempted to determine how much I needed to pay for a few papayas, or I had figure out how to buy movie tickets or how to order at a restaurant. Those moments were scary, but they were also human.

It has me thinking about a time twenty years ago when I got lost in Sao Paulo. I was with my fellow American college students at an outdoor market. We were supposed to meet back together at noon. We had a whole buddy system. But I wandered around, mesmerized the sights, and sounds and smells of the market.

At some point, I lost track of the time. I practiced my memorized lines and paid full price for every fruit I tried; not because I was generous but because I still didn't know how to bargain with people. I glanced at my watch and realized it was still 10:21 – the same as it was before. My watch had stopped working. We had no phones at the time, so there was no way to get ahold of my friends.

I wandered around searching for a clock. Then I panicked when I saw the time. It was 12:30. I ran to the meetup spot, but no one was there. Had they left without me?

For the next ten minutes, I tried to find someone who spoke English. I wanted to know if my friends had left a message with someone. I kept asking questions in my mediocre Portuguese. Nobody knew anything about my friends.

Eventually, I broke down. I sat on a bench and wept. Big tears. Huge convulsions. Snot running out of my nose. I felt so embarrassed by my inability to communicate the most basic conversational Portuguese that I had practiced.

Finally, a woman in her seventies approached me and handed me a water bottle. I reached out to pay her for it, but she waved me off.

I used whatever Portuguese words I knew to explain that I was lost. Our group had a plan. If we ever got truly lost, we would take a bus back to the hotel. I knew the address, but I didn't know how to navigate the bus system. I wasn't even sure where we were. I asked if there was a bus stop nearby.

"I walk there with you," she said in English.

We walked for twenty minutes. I spoke in Portuguese. She spoke in English. We both spoke with our hands.

She explained that her two children both moved to southern California years ago. Her husband had passed away three years ago, but she wasn't lonely. She had lots of friends at her church. Take that back. Sometimes she felt lonely but only sometimes. She apologized for lying. She actually felt very lonely. She misses him every day. She feels guilty that she gets mad at him for leaving her.

She asked about me. I told her that I was a college student from Arizona. I was planning to be a teacher. She told me that was a noble profession. I thanked her. She told me about a teacher she had that was strict but fair and she hated this woman at the time, but she thinks back fondly on this woman. Eventually, we made it back to the bus stop. I gave her a hug and road back to the hotel.

Fast forward to the present day. When I need to ride the bus, I simply type in the directions and an algorithm tells me where to go. I get clear directions with precise time estimations. But I don't get to hear a story. I'm not forced to communicate with my hands. I'm not sure I will ever again leave an interaction in a foreign city feeling grateful for a woman who would take forty minutes outside of her day to help a stranger who was lost and scared. I don't know what world languages will look like in an era of algorithms. My hope, though, is that we can retain the human connection.

CHAPTER 19

INTEGRATING ARTIFICIAL INTELLIGENCE INTO CAREER AND TECHNICAL EDUCATION

Recently, I sat down with a team of teachers at the Entrepreneur-ship and Innovation Center (EIC) in Williamson County, Tennessee. Students have the chance to dive headfirst into entrepreneurship and innovation. They start actual businesses, launch real products, and provide services for the community. Along the way, they receive val-uable CTE credit.

I'm loving this opportunity EIC provides. Students can explore services like lawn care, babysitting, and photography. But they can also tackle global issues like water scarcity. They might start busi-nesses in baking, retail, or automotive. They often launch innovative products that meet genuine needs. By nurturing a spirit of innovation and entrepreneurship, the EIC helps students turn their dreams into reality.

While this program prepares students to be entrepreneurs, I left the day wondering if that's not actually the main goal. Some of these student-created companies are successful. Some not so much. Some of the companies fail to become truly viable and profitable. But I wouldn't call this a failure. There's something deeper at work. Stu-dents learn to think like entrepreneurs. They learn how to take creative risks, iterate in their work, and build empathy with customers. Some students might go on to start companies in the future. Some might work in a specific field or industry and never start their own company. Regardless of the setting, each student will someday bring an entrepreneurial edge to their work.

In a world of rapid change, the traditional view of vocational suc-cess doesn't capture this new reality of work in a world of smart machines. If students learn to think like entrepreneurs, they are the most poised to adapt to a rapidly changing workforce. In other words, this program helps students navigate the maze of a complex world.

In an era of machine learning, CTE programs will need to have elements of entrepreneurial thinking. Students will need to be adapt-able, empathetic, and resilient. Whether students are studying early childhood education or automotive, they will need to engage in au-thentic problem-solving through project-based learning. Along the way, they will discover how A.I. is transforming each industry.

HOW IS A.I. USED IN INDUSTRY?

We can't predict how A.I. will change different professions. We can, however, ask how A.I. is currently transforming professions and consider what those changes mean for CTE programs.

A.I. has been making waves in various industries, and Career and Technical Education (CTE) programs might need to explore how the use of A.I. in their curriculum might better equip students for a workforce with smart machines. Here are some examples of how A.I. is being utilized in different fields:

- **Business and Marketing:** A.I. helps marketers analyze customer behavior and preferences to design personalize marketing campaigns. It's also widely used to provide real-time support through chatbots. At a more systemic level, companies deploy A.I. to improve supply chain management, optimize pricing strategies, and automate administrative tasks. In a marketing class, students might explore the pros and cons of using adaptive A.I. for market research and advertising. In a business class, they might examine how it's changing global economic systems and changing supply chains.

- **Health Sciences:** A.I. is prevalent as a diagnostic tool. It's being used to improve patient care and medical research. By analyzing medical images like MRI scans and X-rays, A.I. helps practitioners identify anomalies and aid in the diagnosis of diseases. A.I. is also being utilized to develop new drugs and therapies. In a health science classes, students might learn about how to use these systems in a way that's ethical and enhances rather than inhibits bedside manner.

- **Information Technology:** This is an industry facing huge changes and potential displacement in areas like coding / programming. A chatbot can do in seconds what a coder does in a day. We'll explore this idea later in the chapter, but technology classes will be a key area for educators to reimagine the curriculum.

- **Agriculture and Natural Resources:** When we think forestry and farming, it might seem that this is a world away from machine learning. However, A.I. is being used to improve crop yields, monitor environmental conditions, and optimize resource management. Farmers use A.I. algorithms to analyze soil and weather data to provide precise recommendations for fertilization and irrigation, while drones equipped with A.I.-powered sensors monitor crop health and detect disease outbreaks. I recently met with a group of students in agriculture education who had visited various farms through FFA (Future Farmworkers of America) and they were shocked by how pervasive A.I. was to the process. This has the potential to reduce food waste and thus help fight climate change.

- **Hospitality and Tourism:** This industry uses A.I. to improve customer experiences and optimize operations. Through A.I.-powered chatbots and virtual assistants, personalized recommendations can be provided, customer inquiries can be answered, and 24/7 support can be given.

- **Engineering and Manufacturing:** Machine learning is transforming product design, optimizing production processes, and improving quality control. A.I. algorithms analyze product data to provide recommendations for design improvements, while A.I.-powered robots and automation systems optimize production lines and reduce costs.

- **Automotive:** Mechanics regularly use A.I. as a part of the diagnostic process. Machine learning helps them determine what's gone wrong and how to fix things in a more efficient way. But A.I. can also help with predictive maintenance. If you've ever gotten a report that says a particular belt will need to be fixed in the next six months, then you've seen how this predictive maintenance works. Mechanics also use A.I. to optimize vehicle performance. By analyzing data from sensors and other sources, A.I. algorithms can identify ways to improve fuel efficiency, reduce emissions, and enhance over-all vehicle performance.

- **Fire and Safety:** In both fire science and law enforcement, A.I. can be used to create training simulations. In firefighting, A.I. can help simulate fire scenarios and provide students with hands-on training in a safe and controlled environment. A.I. algorithms can be used to generate virtual reality scenarios that are realistic and dynamic, adjusting based on the actions of the trainees. Students in CTE classes might also learn how firefighters use A.I.-powered sensors and drones can be used to gather data on the spread of fires, the condition of build-ings, and the location of victims, helping firefighters to make more informed decisions and respond more effectively to emergency situations.

- **Education and Child Development:** Students in early child-hood education classes might use A.I. to learn through simulations or to create individualized plans. A.I. can be used to create interactive educational content that is tailored to the needs and interests of each child.

These are just a few examples. There are so many other trades using A.I. to improve safety, efficiency, and accuracy.

INSTEAD OF ASKING,
"HOW WILL WE USE
AI IN FUTURE JOBS?"
ASK, "HOW ARE YOU
USING AI RIGHT NOW?"

A.I.-powered robots and drones perform dangerous or repetitive tasks like welding and painting, while A.I.-powered software analyzes building plans to identify potential issues before construction begins. A.I.-powered tools improve precision and accuracy in carpentry.

Ultimately, the integration of A.I. into CTE programs will prepare students with the necessary skills to succeed in the workforce and contribute to the growth and innovation of various industries.

This is why industry partnerships are so important. It's one thing to guess how A.I. will transform an industry. It's another thing to have a guest speaker say, "A.I. is changing my job in huge ways." It's one thing to read an article about A.I. in a specific domain. It's another thing to experience A.I. integration firsthand in an internship. If CTE programs want to adapt to the times, they will need to connect with industry partners in significant ways and reimagine their curriculum.

WHAT IF A.I. REPLACES THE JOB?

I recently tested out several different chatbots to see how well it did with coding for Raspberry Pi and Arduino. I used the same prompts I had given to my students. It took the A.I. about 90 seconds to create the kind of code my students used to spend a full week creating – and those were the advanced students who had moved from Scratch video game projects to full-scale programming.

Is coding obsolete, then?

Not exactly.

When I taught middle school STEM, my students would do a 3-week Scratch Video Game Project. Later, in our Genius Hour projects, some students could go deeper into coding while others worked on a documentary or a set of STEM challenges. Several former students have become programmers after taking coding classes at high school and college. But that's still a small percentage of those who learned how to program. If the goal is to prepare students for a job, then I'd failed miserably in our STEM class.

However, even back then, we knew that A.I. would someday write a large portion of the code. And yet, we chose to teach it anyway. So, why bother teaching something so replaceable? Simple. Learning to code isn't about preparing programmers. It's about preparing students for an unpredictable world. It's about developing skills such as mathematical reasoning, logic, problem-solving, systems thinking, iterative thinking, experimentation, curiosity, and creativity.

Is programming the only way to get there? By no means. Students learn many of these skills (and more) when they learn to play an instrument or learn to play chess.

Programming will continue to evolve. Students who learn to code may find themselves using A.I. as a starting point and then modifying the code. Or they might shift into a role of a curator of code. They might find themselves managing multiple A.I. machines creating code that they then combine in creative ways. We don't know what it will look like.

A school subject should never be about preparing for a single job. After all, we do PE even if students don't become professional athletes. We learn history and civics even if students don't become professional historians. They learn math and yet few of them will become mathematicians or statisticians. We learn these things because they make us healthier or because they help us to become better citizens or because we become better critical thinkers.

So, if I taught a STEM class, would we still do coding? Absolutely. But we would also build things out of duct tape and cardboard and learn circuitry and do an empathy-based design project. Because the best way to prepare students for the future is by empowering them in the present.

TRUE, CTE PROGRAMS PREPARE STUDENTS FOR A CAREER. BUT THEY ALSO PREPARE STUDENTS FOR AN UNCERTAIN FUTURE.

PREPARE STUDENTS FOR ANYTHING

For decades, the focus of CTE has been to prepare students for a specific vocation. Someone in an automotive class learns how to work on cars with the hopes of becoming a mechanic. Someone in a culinary class learns the ins and outs of food science with the hopes of becoming a chef or getting a job in restaurant management. A student taking CTE classes in technology might hope to become a programmer or an IT technician in the future. A student might learn the beginnings of welding, plumbing, carpentry, or electrical work with the hopes of moving into trade school and entering one of those professions.

But the thing is, we can't easily predict which jobs A.I. will displace. Every industry is changing, not only in how they use A.I. but in which human skills are necessary given the reality of A.I. We can assume we'll need plumbers and carpenters, but we don't know what these trades might look like in a decade or two. Will the combination of 3D printing and A.I. change home construction? While we can assume most robots won't be able to do plumbing (the more adaptable and hands-on a task, the harder it becomes for a robot to do), we don't know what breakthroughs might occur with A.I. as a plumbing diagnostic tool.

We can't predict how industries will evolve. With automation and A.I., we will continue to see massive changes in many industries.[125] Students will enter a workforce where they might be changing jobs every 5-7 years.[126]

If our students will enter a maze, it doesn't make sense for CTE to prepare students for one narrow job, much less one single discipline. True, students will need the technical skills that students learn in CTE programs. But they'll need to apply these technical skills to multiple jobs in multiple domains.

In his book *Range*, David Epstein explores the benefits of having a wide range of experiences and interests, as opposed to specializing in one area.[127] The book argues that people with diverse backgrounds and interests are often better equipped to solve complex problems and adapt to new situations than those who have focused on one particular field. Being a generalist in several different domains makes you adaptable. This unique combination is what ends up making you a specialist who can adapt to new environments. In other words, by being a generalists in multiple seemingly unrelated fields, students become highly sought after specialists. Their unique combination of skills (their range) is their specialty.

If we want to prepare students for an uncertain future, they'll need a broad set of practical skills from multiple career paths – and this unique set of diverse skills will be the very thing that sets them apart from the crowd.

CTE programs provide an opportunity for students to apply and practice the broader, more universal skills that they will need in a world of smart machines. When students learn how to craft a dish and present it to a real-world context in a timely manner, they learn more than just culinary arts. They learn empathy, communication, problem-solving, and time management. If a student doesn't end up in the restaurant industry, the course wasn't wasted. Those lessons remain relevant forever.

As we think about A.I. and CTE, we might need a shift in mindset from singular pathways and toward a maze of possibilities. We don't need to abandon the practical trade skills students learn. But we need to recognize that they will apply these skills in creative ways within contexts that we can't even predict.

CHAPTER 20
THE CHANGING ROLE OF
TEACHERS

While most of this book has focused on what A.I. means for students, let's explore what A.I. means for teachers. At the start of this book, I shared the story that left me asking, "Will smart machines replace me?"

The obvious answer is, "No way!"

The more nuanced answer is, "No, but . . . it will change the way I do my job."

Last week, I used the latest version of ChatGPT to automate many of the jobs that I used to do as a middle school teacher. For example, I asked it to write a classroom newsletter. For this prompt, I decided to go with a fictional fourth grade classroom.

I typed in, "Write a classroom newsletter for a 4th grade classroom. It needs to include a summary of what we have done in class this week (extreme weather events, reading the book *Alma and How She Got Her Name*, fractions, dividing with remainders). We also need parent volunteers to chaperone the field trip on April 12th. Remind parents and guardians that homework is optional."

The result was decent, but it was a little too short. So, I asked for it to expand on the initial newsletter. It did well with the length but struggled with the nuance of the term "guardians," so I had it change the language to "families" and to "adult chaperone." I then asked it to add a section about how students might practice the math skills at home. This was the result.

Dear Families,

Exciting things are happening in our class! This week, we have been exploring the topic of extreme weather events and how they can impact communities. We have been learning about different types of weather, such as hurricanes, tornadoes, and droughts, and discussing how they can affect people's lives. We also finished reading the book *Alma and How She Got Her Name* by Jacqueline Woodson and had meaningful discussions about the themes and characters in the book. The students were able to identify and relate to the main character's experiences, and they enjoyed discussing how they would have felt if they were in the same situation.

In math, we have been diving deeper into the concept of fractions, and we have been practicing dividing with remainders. The students have been working on understanding the relationship between fractions and division, and they have been applying their knowledge to solve real-world problems.

To help children continue to practice math at home, they can use real-life examples like cooking and timing events. For example, they can measure ingredients when cooking, practice timing how long it takes to complete a task, or even divide up a pizza into equal slices.

We are excited to announce that we will be taking a field trip on April 12th, and we would greatly appreciate the support of adult chaperones to join us. The field trip will be an excellent opportunity for the students to apply their learning and have a hands-on experience. If you are available and interested in chaperoning, please let us know.

Also, as a reminder, homework is optional, and we encourage students to read for pleasure outside of class. Reading is a great way to improve vocabulary, comprehension, and critical thinking skills.

As always, if you have any questions or concerns, please don't hesitate to reach out to us. We are always here to help and support your child's learning.

Thank you,

[Your Name]
[4th Grade Teacher]

Grade: A-

The result was high quality. The tone was professional, readable, and practical.

How a teacher might use it:

A teacher could begin with this newsletter and then revise it to capture their voice. This teacher might add a touch of humor or an inside joke. To make it more context specific, students could add some sections to the newsletter and perhaps even some photos of the class at work (with written permission and photo releases).

One option would be to give the chatbot a set of previous newsletters and ask it to mimic your own writing style. While it doesn't do a perfect job, the initial results are a solid start that you can edit.

From here, I automated several more jobs and gave a score for each task. My score is admittedly subjective. My criteria was simply, "How well does this work?" followed by "Does this save me time?"

Task 2:

Generate 10 project ideas for 4th grade math

Answer:
when I asked it to go with 4th grade level project-based learning ideas for math, things fell apart:

- Investigating different ways to make a whole number using fractions, and creating a class poster or book.
- Measuring and comparing the weight, length, and volume of different objects and creating a graph to show the results.
- Creating and solving word problems that involve addition and subtraction with multi-digit numbers.
- Building and measuring 3-D shapes such as pyramids, spheres, and cones, and finding their surface area and volume.
- Creating a class calendar and solving time-related word problems.
- Organizing a class store and using money math skills to make change and balance the cash register.
- Planning and carrying out a class survey, and creating a graph to represent the data.
- Creating a game that involves using place value and number sense to solve problems.
- Investigating different types of quadrilaterals and their properties.
- Creating and solving multiplication and division word problems using arrays, area models, and other strategies.

Grade: D

Aside from the game and the class store, these are all activities, not projects. None of these fit the PBL criteria of learning *through* the project. This doesn't mean that the ideas are bad. A teacher could incorporate these ideas into a larger PBL unit or even shorter design sprints. But it's a reminder that teachers have past experiences and pedagogical knowledge that an A.I. simply doesn't have.

Task 3: Make a lesson plan

I gave it the prompt, "Make a lesson plan about the Industrial Revolution for a 7th grade classroom." The result was a somewhat traditional Gradual Release styled social studies lesson:

The A.I. Roadmap

Lesson Title: Understanding the Industrial Revolution
Grade Level: 7th grade
Objectives:

- Students will understand the causes and effects of the Industrial Revolution.
- Students will be able to analyze primary and secondary sources to gather information about the Industrial Revolution.
- Students will be able to explain the impact of the Industrial Revolution on society, economy and the environment.

Materials:

- Textbook or articles about the Industrial Revolution
- Primary source documents such as letters, diary entries, and photographs from the Industrial Revolution
- Computer with internet access

Procedure:

1. Introduction (10 minutes): Begin the lesson by asking students what they know about the Industrial Revolution. Write their responses on the board. Ask them to share any prior knowledge they have about the topic.
2. Direct Instruction (20 minutes): Provide students with a brief overview of the causes and effects of the Industrial Revolution. Use a textbook or articles to provide background information on the technological advancements, economic changes, and social impacts of the Industrial Revolution.
3. Group Activity (30 minutes): Divide the class into small groups and provide each group with primary source documents from the Industrial Revolution. These could include letters, diary entries, or photographs. Have each group analyze the documents and create a summary of the information they have gathered.
4. Class Discussion (20 minutes): Have each group share their findings with the class. Encourage students to ask questions and make connections between the primary sources and the information from the direct instruction.
5. Independent Research (20 minutes): Assign students to research a specific aspect of the Industrial Revolution, such as the impact on the environment or the working conditions of factory workers. Have them use the internet to find sources and take notes.
6. Conclusion (10 minutes): Have students share their findings with the class. Summarize the main points of the lesson and ask students to

reflect on the impact of the Industrial Revolution on society, economy, and the environment.

Assessment:

- Students will be assessed on their ability to analyze primary sources and make connections to the information provided during the direct instruction.
- Students will be assessed on their ability to explain the impact of the Industrial Revolution on society, economy and the environment through the independent research and class discussion.
- A written report or presentation can also be used to evaluate their understanding of the topic.

I next had it reduce the lesson down to sixty minutes. Although it took a minute, the revision was practical and feasible. I can see teachers using ChatGPT to revise lessons to meet shorter or longer time frames.

When I asked it to come up with ELL accommodations, it added:

- Provide a vocabulary list with key terms related to the Industrial Revolution, and pre-teach these words before the lesson.
- Use visual aids and pictures to help ELL students understand the concepts and ideas related to the Industrial Revolution.
- Use graphic organizers to help ELL students organize and make sense of information.
- Provide a simplified version of the primary sources documents or use captioned videos to provide the same information.
- Allow ELL students to use a translator or dictionary during the group activity and independent research.
- Pair ELL students with a fluent English speaking peer during group work or independent research.
- Provide extra time for ELL students to complete tasks and assignments related to the lesson.
- Provide additional scaffolding and support for ELL students during the class discussion.
- Encourage the use of L1 (first language) for ELL students when appropriate, for example, when explaining difficult concepts or when providing feedback on their work.

Grade: B-

Overall, the lesson was somewhere around a B-. It was a solid start but not great. ChatGPT did a great job with the alignment the progression. It had a clear and logical flow. Unfortunately, it was a bit boring.

This is a decent starting place for a lesson, but it lacks engagement, and it doesn't include enough individual, peer, and small group processing time. If I were teaching about the Industrial Revolution, I might do a mock factory simulation to tap into students' prior knowledge and boost engagement. I would also front-load vocabulary at the beginning and incorporate this visually into the simulation. I would break up direct instruction to have some cooperative learning strategies, including some think-pair-shares and round robin activities.

Again, there's the sense that ChatGPT can create a basic, slightly boring, lesson plan. My job would be to modify this with higher engagement and a knowledge of my students. I'd add my own expertise in breaking up tasks to reduce cognitive overload and the result would be better than something purely A.I.-generated.

A FEW MORE EXAMPLES

The following are a few more tasks that I attempted to automate:

- **Creating leveled readers (A):** I was impressed by the way it created leveled reading materials for a rotating reading activity.
- **Creating directions for a simulation (A):** I began with my own idea of a simulation game / activity and then asked it to create step-by-step directions and handouts for students. The result was impressive.
- **Breaking down a student project into a set of tasks with clear deadlines (A-):** The ability to use it as a planning tool was impressive. We covered this idea previously in the PBL chapter.
- **Creating skill-based optional homework (B+):** It was amazingly fast at generating a skill practice worksheet for science. I would still need to do all the formatting, but this was a quality starting place.
- **Making a rubric for a presentation (B):** The rubric was good, but it focused too much on the finished product and not the process or really the learning. Even when I prompted it to change the focus, the generative A.I. still struggled.
- **Creating vocabulary (B):** The vocabulary definitions were solid and the sample sentences were decent. But I would still need to modify this based on my students' prior knowledge.
- **Creating ELL accommodations (C+):** The sentence stems were not as practical as I had hoped, and they required a lot of tweaking and changes. With additional training and examples, I'm guessing I could get the chatbot to do well.

WHAT DOES THIS MEAN?

In most areas, the A.I. won't replace a teaching task entirely. However, it can function as a solid starting place. It gives you something akin to a template that you can then modify.

I get excited about the ways that A.I. might automate some of the boring, repetitive tasks we do on a regular basis to free us up to spend more time doing the work we find most meaningful. Consider the example of an A.I. reading fluency screener. If an A.I. can screen for fluency and test students on phonics and blending, the algorithm can identify key areas where students need more instruction. The teacher is then freed up to spend more time providing small group and individual instruction in a way that saves time.

Artificial Intelligence has the potential to work as a personal assistant for teachers. A.I. might generate parent newsletters or take your own lesson outline and turn it into a full lesson plan. You might end up using A.I. to create rubrics or design leveled reading for your learning centers. You might use it to develop project plans and make predictions on how long things take.

In this sense, the A.I. might free you up to do more human-centered jobs. So, you might do less assessment but more one-on-one conferences. You might use it for that newsletter, but you'll add your own personal flair with personal references and your own sense of humor. In other words, you'll take the vanilla and make it into something that is uniquely yours.

YOUR HUMANITY, WITH ALL ITS IMPERFECTIONS, IS A GIFT TO YOUR STUDENTS

There's a danger, though, in allowing the A.I. to do too many aspects of our jobs. The false promise of Techno Futurism is that the perfect machine can replace the imperfect teacher. However, our imperfections are part of what makes learning authentic for students.

A few months ago, a former student of mine reached out to me and said, "Mr. Spencer, you're why I became a teacher."

"Thank you so much," I answered. Then I asked, "What was it about me that you remember so much?"

"I think it was when you yelled at our class, she said.

My heart sank. This was the memory? Me yelling at a group of sixth graders.

"I still cringe when I think of those moments," I answered. "It was a hard year and even now I still feel embarrassed by the fact that I yelled at your class."

"Don't be embarrassed," she answered. "I think it happened once or twice that year but when it did, you apologized. Like a real apology. Not an 'I'm sorry you made me do that.' You didn't blame us even though we had been awful. You owned it. And you were the first adult in my life that ever apologized to me."

"Wow," I answered.

"Don't get me wrong. We did some really cool projects. And that year was when I fell in love with reading and writing. But those apologies? They stuck with me."

This was a reminder that our humanity, as imperfect as it may be, is a gift to our students. In an age of A.I., our students still need a human to listen and empathize; to experiment and adapt; to make mistakes and apologize. They will need a guide who can build a relationship and help them navigate a complex world.

Dr. John Spencer

OUR STUDENTS WILL NEED A MAP

Our students will navigate the maze of an uncertain future. There will be no instruction manual. We will figure things out as we go. There will be no playbook. In fact, the rules will change constantly. But we, as educators can help our students navigate this uncertain future.

Part of this navigation will involve thinking wisely about when to use A.I. It will involve thinking critically about how A.I. is changing our world, including how we engage in creativity or what this looks like for information literacy.

It might involve navigating the changing terrain of the actual school subjects. Much of this navigation will involve developing critical human skills that machines cannot do. It will involve finding unusual routes through a complex maze.

Here's where our flawed humanity becomes a gift. As imperfect guides in a changing world, we can model what it means to hit a dead end and find a new route. We can demonstrate creativity and divergent thinking when faced with barriers. We can show humility when we lead the class into a dead end and we say, "I messed up here." We can show empathy as we run into other travelers in this changing terrain. In other words, we can be boldly human in an age of smart machines.

In the end, there is not one single A.I. roadmap. There are many maps filled with endless opportunities. As educators, we will all be cartographers mapping out new possibilities for our students. We will be guides helping students learn how to use A.I. wisely and ethically. We will provide experiences that help them use A.I. in a human-centered way. But we will also step back at times and empower our students with a sense of ownership over their journey, trusting that they will find a way to build a better future.

STUDENTS WILL NEED TO

OWN

THEIR JOURNEY

ENDNOTES

[1] Turing, Alan. "Computing Machinery and Intelligence." Mind 59, no. 236 (1950): 433-460. doi:10.1093/mind/LIX.236.433.
It should be noted that Turing never called it the Turing Test. It was the "imitation game." Also, many computer scientists and A.I. experts have developed more complex versions of the Turing Test that delve deeper into human cognition and include aspects of the affective realm.

[2] Etherington, Darrell. "OpenA.I.'s ChatGPT Shows Why Implementation is Key with Generative A.I." TechCrunch, December 2, 2022, accessed December 2, 2022, https://techcrunch.com/2022/12/02/openais-chatgpt-shows-why-implementation-is-key-with-generative-ai/.

[3] Bek, Nate and Taylor Soper. "OpenA.I.'s ChatGPT bot sparks excitement and concern from investors, entrepreneurs, researchers." GeekWire, December 5, 2022, 12:25 PM, accessed April 11, 2023, https://www.geekwire.com/2022/openais-chatgpt-bot-sparks-excitement-and-concern-from-investors-entrepreneurs-researchers/.

[4] Milmo, Dan. "ChatGPT: 100 Million Users for OpenA.I.'s Fastest Growing App." The Guardian, February 2, 2023, 15:46 EST, accessed April 11, 2023, https://www.theguardian.com/technology/2023/feb/02/chatgpt-100-million-users-open-ai-fastest-growing-app.

[5] This is not meant as an endorsement of using A.I. for personal fitness. This example reflects my personal experiences and should not be considered a substitute for professional advice regarding health, fitness, mental health, or medical issues. Please note that I am not a registered dietitian or medical doctor. If you require assistance or have any health-related concerns, please seek advice from a qualified professional. Before beginning any new diet or exercise regimen, ALWAYS consult with your medical doctor(s).

[6] Sharma A, Virmani T, Pathak V, Sharma A, Pathak K, Kumar G, Pathak D. Artificial Intelligence-Based Data-Driven Strategy to Accelerate Research, Development, and Clinical Trials of COVID Vaccine. Biomed Res Int. 2022 Jul 6;2022:7205241. doi: 10.1155/2022/7205241. PMID: 35845955; PMCID: PMC9279074.

[7] Some great points about the unintended consequences can be found here: Harrison, Maggie. "A.I. CEO: GPT-4 Super Dangerous." Futurism. March 16, 2023. https://futurism.com/the-byte/ai-ceo-gpt-4-super-dangerous.

[8] Future of Life Institute. "An Open Letter: Research Priorities for Robust and Beneficial Artificial Intelligence." Accessed April 11, 2023. https://futureof-life.org/open-letter/pause-giant-ai-experiments/.

There's a great commentary on this by Michael Wooldridge on the Patented Podcast: https://access.historyhit.com/patented/videos/patented-ai. He argues that it's nearly impossible to slow down an invention.

[9] Hosanagar, Kartik. A Human's Guide to Machine Intelligence. New York: Penguin Press, 2019.

[10] There's been a huge push toward so-called "smart cities" that employ A.I. on a largescale, interconnected way. For a glimpse of what this looks like, you might want to check out what Alibaba is doing in China. It feels both amazing and terrifying.

"Alibaba Sets Up A.I. Labs at Two Prestigious Chinese Universities, Washington." South China Morning Post, December 22, 2021. Accessed April 11, 2023. https://www.scmp.com/tech/big-tech/article/3193012/alibaba-sets-ai-labs-two-prestigious-chinese-universities-washington.

[11] McCarthy, John, Marvin Minsky, Nathaniel Rochester, and Claude Shannon. "A Proposal for the Dartmouth Summer Research Project on Artificial Intelligence, August 31, 1955." A.I. Magazine 27, no. 4 (2006): 12-14. Accessed April 11, 2023. https://www.aaai.org/ojs/index.php/aimagazine/article/view/1904/1802.

[12] For more on this topic, check out:
Vincent, James (December 5, 2022). "A.I.-generated answers temporarily banned on coding Q&A site Stack Overflow". The Verge. Archived from the original on January 17, 2023. Retrieved December 5, 2022.

[13] Heikkilä, Melissa. "How OpenA.I. is trying to make ChatGPT safer and less biased." MIT Technology Review, February 21, 2023. https://www.technolo-gyreview.com/2023/02/21/1068893/how-openai-is-trying-to-make-chatgpt-safer-and-less-biased/.

[14] Alba, Davey. "ChatGPT, Open A.I.'s Chatbot, Is Spitting Out Biased, Sexist Results." Bloomberg News, December 8, 2022. https://www.bloomberg.com/news/newsletters/2022-12-08/chatgpt-open-ai-s-chatbot-is-spitting-out-biased-sexist-results.

[15] There's a great podcast episode about this from 99% Invisible: "You've Got Enron Mail." 99% Invisible, episode 404, directed by Roman Mars, December 7, 2021, podcast audio, 33:51. https://99percentinvisible.org/episode/youve-got-enron-mail/.

[16] Simonite, Tom. "How to Understand Artificial Intelligence." Wired, February 8, 2023, 7:00 AM EST. Accessed April 11, 2023. https://www.wired.com/story/guide-artificial-intelligence/.

[17] As early as 2016, certain programmers were already saying that coding was not "the new literacy." Check out this article:

Farag, Basel. "Please Don't Learn to Code." TechCrunch, May 10, 2016, 5:00 PM PDT. https://techcrunch.com/2016/05/10/please-dont-learn-to-code/.

[18] Kurasińska, Lidia, and Michał Frąk. "Will Artificial Intelligence Replace Developers?" STX Next, accessed April 11, 2023. https://www.stxnext.com/blog/will-artificial-intelligence-replace-developers/.

[19] For a great take on the dangers of techno futurism, check out both of these books by Larry Cuban:

Cuban, Larry. Teachers and Machines: The Classroom Use of Technology Since 1920. New York: Teachers College Press, 1986.

Cuban, Larry. Oversold and Underused: Computers in the Classroom. Cambridge, MA: Harvard University Press, 2001.

[20] https://www.youtube.com/watch?v=qd-Nk2sB-vA

[21] Umejima, Keita, Takuya Ibaraki, Takahiro Yamazaki, and Kuniyoshi L. Sakai. "Paper Notebooks vs. Mobile Devices: Brain Activation Differences During Memory Retrieval." Frontiers in Behavioral Neuroscience, Volume 15 (2021): https://doi.org/10.3389/fnbeh.2021.634158.

---

[22] Morrison, Karin, Mark Church, and Ron Ritchhart. Making Thinking Visible: How to Promote Engagement, Understanding, and Independence for All Learners. San Francisco: Jossey-Bass, 2011.

[23] Hertz, Mary Beth [@mbteach]. "I'm following the GPT3 chatbot conversations closely, especially those that are open-minded & understand that academic surveillance is not the answer. I also hope folks see the ableism involved in requiring handwritten exams & I hope we've learned our lesson re: Proctorio..." Twitter, December 8, 2022, 4:45 PM. https://twitter.com/mbteach/status/1601015128702726144.

[24] COPPA stands for the Children's Online Privacy Protection Act, which is a United States federal law that was enacted in 1998. The law is designed to protect the online privacy of children under the age of 13 by regulating the collection, use, and disclosure of their personal information by online services and websites.

Under COPPA, website operators must obtain verifiable parental consent before collecting, using, or disclosing personal information from children. The law also requires website operators to post a clear and comprehensive online privacy policy, provide notice to parents about their information practices, and give parents the right to access and delete their child's personal information.
COPPA is enforced by the Federal Trade Commission (FTC) and includes significant fines for violations. In addition, the FTC regularly updates its guidance on how to comply with the law to reflect changes in technology and online services.

[25] CIPA stands for the Children's Internet Protection Act, which is a United States federal law that was enacted in 2000. The law is designed to promote online safety for children in public schools and libraries by requiring them to implement internet safety policies and technology protection measures.

Under CIPA, schools and libraries that receive federal funding for internet access are required to have an internet safety policy that includes measures to protect against access to harmful or obscene content, as well as online predators and cyberbullying. In addition, they must implement technology protection measures, such as filters or blocking software, to restrict access to inappropriate content.

CIPA also requires schools and libraries to educate minors about appropriate online behavior, including interacting with other individuals on social networking websites and in chat rooms, and the potential risks associated with online activity.
CIPA is enforced by the Federal Communications Commission (FCC) and includes significant penalties for noncompliance, including loss of federal funding. See: www.ftc.gov/enforcement/rules/rulemaking-regulatory-reform-proceedings/childrens-online-privacy-protection-rule.

[26] Spencer, John. Vintage Innovation: Leveraging Retro Tools and Classic Ideas to Design Deeper Learning Experiences. Blend Education, 2019.

[27] Huang, Tina. "Why Computer-Assisted Humans Are The Best Chess Players And What That Means For Technology Operations." Forbes Technology Council. Forbes, January 7, 2022. Accessed [date]. URL: https://www.forbes.com/sites/forbestechcouncil/2022/01/07/why-computer-assisted-humans-are-the-best-chess-players-and-what-that-means-for-technology-operations/?sh=62f9756d14e0

[28] Merisotis, Jamie. Human Work in the Age of Smart Machines. Brookings Institution Press, 2020.

[29] Spencer, John, and A.J. Juliani. Empower: What Happens When Students Own Their Learning. IMPress, 2017.

[30] Bershidsky, Leonid. "The 19th-century health scare that told women to worry about "bicycle face"." Vox, July 8, 2014. Accessed April 11, 2023. https://www.vox.com/2014/7/8/5880931/the-19th-century-health-scare-that-told-women-to-worry-about-bicycle.

[31] Theule, Larissa. Born to ride: A story about bicycle face. Abrams, 2019.

[32] Bendix, Aria. "When the Telephone Was Dangerous." The Atlantic, September 18, 2015. Accessed April 11, 2023. https://www.theatlantic.com/technology/archive/2015/09/when-the-telephone-was-dangerous/626742/.

[33] Note that this isn't the same as Gartner's Hype Cycle, which is more about the hype, disappointment, and acceptance of new technology: https://www.gartner.com/en

[34] Schultz, Jaime. "The physical is political: Women's suffrage, pilgrim hikes and the public sphere." The International Journal of the History of Sport 27, no. 7 (2010): 1133-1153.

[35] Sunesti, Yuyun. "Media and Modernity: the Role of the Printing Press in the Modernization of Western Society." KOMUNIKA: Jurnal Dakwah dan Komunikasi 5, no. 2 (2011): 291-301.

[36] Spohr, Dominic. "Fake news and ideological polarization: Filter bubbles and selective exposure on social media." Business information review 34, no. 3 (2017): 150-160.

[37] For a deeper dive on this subject, check out Philip Tetlock's work on this subject:

Tetlock, Philip E., and Dan Gardner. Superforecasting: The art and science of prediction. Random House, 2016.

[38] Fliess, Sue. Robots, Robots Everywhere! Illustrated by Bob Staake. New York: Golden Books, 2013.

[39] Dyckman, Ame. Boy and Bot. Illustrated by Dan Yaccarino. New York: Knopf Books for Young Readers, 2012.

[40] Dick, Philip K. Do Androids Dream of Electric Sheep? New York: Ballantine Books, 1968.

[41] Gibson, William. Neuromancer. New York: Ace Books, 1984.

[42] Asimov, Isaac. I, Robot. New York: Gnome Press, 1950.

[43] Meyer, Marissa. Cinder. New York: Feiwel and Friends, 2012.

[44] Ishiguro, Kazuo. Klara and the Sun. New York: Alfred A. Knopf, 2021.

[45] Spencer, John. "Ben Farrell's Surprising Approach to Students Using ChatGPT." Creative Classroom podcast, April 11, 2023.

[46] Zhou, Li, Jianfeng Gao, Di Li, and Heung-Yeung Shum. "The Design and Implementation of XiaoIce, an Empathetic Social Chatbot." arXiv:1812.08989 [cs.HC], December 21, 2018.

[47] Gates, Bill. "My Advice for China's Students." Gates Notes, accessed September 19, 2019. https://www.gatesnotes.com/Education/My-Advice-to-China-Students.

[48] I struggle here with the use of the word "she" for a bot that is not a human. My reason for using it here is that it reflects the deliberately gendered language that Microsoft has used to describe the bot.

[49] Wakefield, Jane. "Microsoft chatbot is taught to swear on Twitter." BBC News, March 24, 2016. Accessed March 25, 2016. http://www.bbc.com/news/technology-35890188.

[50] Mason, Paul. "The racist hijacking of Microsoft's chatbot shows how the internet teems with hate." The Guardian, March 29, 2016. Accessed April 11, 2023. https://www.theguardian.com/commentisfree/2016/mar/29/racist-hijacking-microsofts-chatbot-shows-internet-teems-with-hate.

[51] Bright, Peter. "Tay, the neo-Nazi millennial chatbot, gets autopsied." Ars Technica, March 26, 2016. Accessed March 27, 2016. https://arstechnica.com/information-technology/2016/03/tay-the-neo-nazi-millennial-chatbot-gets-autopsied/.

[52] Allyn, Bobby. "Microsoft's new A.I. chatbot has been saying some 'crazy and unhinged things'." NPR, March 2, 2023. Accessed April 11, 2023. https://www.npr.org/2023/03/02/972377062/microsofts-new-ai-chatbot-has-been-saying-some-crazy-and-unhinged-things.

[53] Bing's chatbot apparently named me as one of its enemies and accused me of rejecting its love after I wrote an article about it
Sindhu Sundar Feb 26, 2023, 4:02 AM

[54] Salah, Mohammed, Hussam Alhalbusi, Maria Mohd Ismail, and Fadi Abdelfattah. "Chatting with ChatGPT: Decoding the Mind of Chatbot Users and Unveiling the Intricate Connections between User Perception, Trust and Stereotype Perception on Self-Esteem and Psychological Well-being." (2023).

[55] Müller, Lea, Jens Mattke, Christian Maier, Tim Weitzel, and Heinrich Graser. "Chatbot acceptance: A latent profile analysis on individuals' trust in conversational agents." In Proceedings of the 2019 on Computers and People Research Conference, pp. 35-42. 2019.

[56] Van Dijck, José. "Television 2.0: YouTube and the emergence of Homecasting." Creativity, Ownership and Collaboration in the Digital Age, Cambridge, Massachusetts Institute of Technology (2007): 27-29.

[57] Spohr, Dominic. "Fake news and ideological polarization: Filter bubbles and selective exposure on social media." Business information review 34, no. 3 (2017): 150-160.

[58] Barthel, Michael, Amy Mitchell, and Jesse Holcomb. "Many Americans Believe Fake News Is Sowing Confusion: 23% say they have shared a made-up news story – either knowingly or not." Pew Research Center, December 15, 2016. Accessed April 11, 2023. https://www.pewresearch.org/politics/2016/12/15/many-americans-believe-fake-news-is-sowing-confusion/.

[59] Spector, Carrie. "High school students are unprepared to judge the credibility of information on the internet, according to Stanford researchers." Stanford Graduate School of Education, November 18, 2019. Accessed April 11, 2023. https://ed.stanford.edu/news/high-school-students-are-unprepared-judge-credibility-information-internet-according-stanford.

[60] Wineburg, Sam, and Sarah McGrew. "Evaluating information: The cornerstone of civic online reasoning." (2016).

[61] "Deepfake." Grammarist, accessed April 11, 2023, https://grammarist.com/new-words/deepfake/.

[62] Kietzmann, J., Lee, L. W., McCarthy, I. P., & Kietzmann, T. C. "Deepfakes: Trick or treat?" Business Horizons 63, no. 2 (2020): 135-146. doi:10.1016/j.bushor.2019.11.006.

[63] Doerr, Helen M. "How Can I Find a Pattern in this Random Data?: The Convergence of Multiplicative and Probabilistic Reasoning." The Journal of Mathematical Behavior 18, no. 4 (2000): 431-454.

---

[64] Malcolm Gladwell did a great job exploring this topic in-depth in his book Talking to Strangers.
Gladwell, M. (2019). Talking to strangers: What we should know about the people we don't know. Little, Brown.

[65] Modjeski, Morgan. "Saskatchewan professor starts website to help catfish victims find answers." Saskatoon StarPhoenix, February 11, 2016.

[66] This is taken from my podcast episode: Spencer, John. "Dr. Alec Couros on Redefining Information Literacy In An Era of A.I." Creative Classroom podcast, March 13, 2023.

[67] Caulfield, M. (2017a). Web literacy for student fact-checkers...and other people who care about facts. Pressbooks. Retrieved March 2, 2021, from https://webliteracy.pressbooks.com/.

[68] Caulfield, Mike. "Information Literacy for Mortals. PIL Provocation Series. Volume 1, Number 5." Project Information Literacy (2021).

[69] Blakeslee, Sarah. "The CRAAP test." Loex Quarterly 31, no. 3 (2004): 4.

[70] https://hapgood.us/2018/09/14/a-short-history-of-craap/

[71] https://hapgood.us/2019/02/04/attention-is-the-scarcity/

[72] Fielding, Jennifer A. "Rethinking CRAAP: Getting students thinking like fact-checkers in evaluating web sources." C&RL News 80, no. 11 (December 2019): 620-622. doi:10.5860/crln.80.11.620.

[73] Fister, Barbara; MacMillan, Margy (May 31, 2019). "Mike Caulfield: Truth Is in the Network: Smart Talk Interview, no. 31". projectinfolit.org. Project Information Literacy. Archived from the original on 2019-08-06. Retrieved 2019-06-14.

[74] LaGarde, J., & Hudgins, D. (2021). Developing Digital Detectives: Essential Lessons for Discerning Fact from Fiction in the 'Fake News' Era. International Society for Technology in Education.

[75] For a deeper dive into this, check out:

IBM, and Institute of Culinary Education. Cognitive Cooking with Chef Watson: Recipes for Innovation from IBM & the Institute of Culinary Education. Hardcover – April 14, 2015.

[76] Goyache, Felix, Antonio Bahamonde, Jaime Alonso, S. López, J. J. Del Coz, J. R. Quevedo, Josr Ranilla et al. "The usefulness of artificial intelligence techniques to assess subjective quality of products in the food industry." Trends in Food Science & Technology 12, no. 10 (2001): 370-381.

[77] Kumar, Indrajeet, Jyoti Rawat, Noor Mohd, and Shahnawaz Husain. "Opportunities of artificial intelligence and machine learning in the food industry." Journal of Food Quality 2021 (2021): 1-10.

[78] Spencer, John. "Seven Stages in Moving from Consuming to Creating." John Spencer, 26 October 2018, https://www.spencerauthor.com/seven-stages/.

[79] Del Signore, John. "Ira Glass, This American Life." Gothamist, 5 Oct. 2007, https://gothamist.com/news/ira-glass-this-american-life.

[80] Mathur, Atreya. "Art-istic or Art-ificial? Ownership and copyright concerns in A.I.-generated artwork." Center for Art Law, November 21, 2022. https://itsartlaw.org/2022/11/21/artistic-or-artificial-ai/#post-5406-footnote-18.

[81] Guadamuz, Andres. "Artificial Intelligence and Copyright." WIPO Magazine, October 2017.

[82] United States Copyright Office. "A Recent Entrance to Paradise." Copyright Review Board. Retrieved April 11, 2023, from https://www.copyright.gov/rulings-filings/review-board/docs/a-recent-entrance-to-paradise.pdf.

[83] Juliani, A. J. (2023, March 23). Can artificial intelligence help us empower students? [Blog post]. Retrieved from https://www.ajjuliani.com/blog/ai-empowering-learners

[84] There are many different PBL models out there and we will not delve into the specific differences between each one. For some background on the components of PBL, see:

Ertmer, P. A., & Simons, K. D. (2006). Jumping the PBL implementation hurdle: Supporting the efforts of K–12 teachers. Interdisciplinary Journal of Problem-Based Learning, 1(1), 40-54.

Jones, B. F., Rasmussen, C. M., & Moffitt, M. C. (1997). Real-life problem solving: A collaborative approach to interdisciplinary learning. Washington, DC: American Psychological Association.

Thomas, J. W., & Mergendoller, J. R. (2000). Managing project-based learning: Principles from the field. Paper presented at the Annual Meeting of the American Educational Research Association, New Orleans.

[85] Kaechele, M., & Ragatz, M. (2022). Pulse of PBL: Cultivating Equity Through Social Emotional Learning. Blend Education.

[86] Anderson, Meg. "How Social-Emotional Learning Became a Frontline in the Battle Against CRT." All Things Considered, NPR, 26 September 2022, https://www.npr.org/2022/09/26/1124082878/how-social-emotional-learning-became-a-frontline-in-the-battle-against-crt.

[87] CASEL. "What Is the CASEL Framework?" CASEL, https://casel.org/what-is-sel/casel-framework/.

[88] Kingston, Sally. "Project Based Learning & Student Achievement: What Does the Research Tell Us? PBL Evidence Matters, Volume 1, No. 1." Buck institute for education (2018).

[89] Xinmei Shen, China is Putting Surveillance Cameras in Plenty of Schools, TECH IN ASIA (Jan. 22, 2019), https://www.techinasia.com/china-putting-surveillance-cameras-plenty-schools.

[90] Rachel England, Chinese School Uses Facial Recognition to Make Kids Pay Attention, ENGADGET (May 17, 2018), https://www.engadget.com/2018/05/17/chinese-school-facial-recognition-kids-attention/.

[91] I recognize that the "reading wars" have become contentious with articles about the "Science of Reading." To be clear, my students still did systematic work in phonemic awareness, phonics, and blending. However, the issue was

less about decoding text and more about comprehension, critical thinking, and reading endurance.

[92] Campbell, Laurie O., Cassandra Howard, Glenn W. Lambie, and Xueying Gao. "The efficacy of a computer-adaptive reading program on grade 5 students' reading achievement scores." Education and Information Technologies 27, no. 6 (2022): 8147-8163.

[93] The citation for Vygotsky is
Vygotsky, L.S. (1978). Mind in society: The development of higher psychological processes. London: Harvard University Press.
However, it should be noted that he died long before then.

[94] Wood, D. J., Bruner, J. S., & Ross, G. (1976). The role of tutoring in problem solving. Journal of Child Psychiatry and Psychology, 17(2), 89-100.

[95] Dweck, Carol S. Mindset: The New Psychology of Success. New York: Ballantine Books, 2006.

[96] Postman, N. (1985). The disappearance of childhood. Childhood Education, 61(4), 286-293.

[97] Rose, David. "Universal design for learning." Journal of Special Education Technology 15, no. 4 (2000): 47-51.

[98] https://www.cast.org/about/board/david-rose

[99] A Great summary of this can be found here:

Zumbrun, J. (2023, February 10). ChatGPT Needs Some Help With Math Assignments. The Wall Street Journal. https://www.wsj.com/articles/chatgpt-needs-some-help-with-math-assignments-11645458000

Note that ChatGPT-4 has performed better than previous generations but there is still a lag in performance with procedural math.

[100] For more on this idea, check out:
Meyer, Dan. "Informed or Not: The Distorted Treatment of Applied Mathematics in Math Curricula and Its Effect on Students." science (2000): 21.

[101] Rittel, Horst W.J., and Melvin M. Webber. "Dilemmas in a General Theory of Planning." Policy Sciences 4, no. 2 (1973): 155-69. doi:10.1007/bf01405730. [Reprinted in Cross, N., ed. (1984). Developments in Design Methodology. Chichester, England: John Wiley & Sons. pp. 135–144.]

[102] Miller, Matt. A.I. for Educators: Learning Strategies, Teacher Efficiencies, and a Vision for an Artificial Intelligence Future. Ditch That Textbook, March 16, 2023.

[103] https://ditchthattextbook.com/ai/

[104] Morrison, Karin, Mark Church, and Ron Ritchhart. Making Thinking Visible: How to Promote Engagement, Understanding, and Independence for All Learners. San Francisco: Jossey-Bass, 2011.

[105] https://www.youtube.com/channel/UCJkMlOu7faDgqh4PfzbpLdg

[106] Enfield, Mark, Edward L. Smith, and David J. Grueber. ""A sketch is like a sentence": Curriculum structures that support teaching epistemic practices of science." Science Education 92, no. 4 (2008): 608-630.

This was explored recently in a dissertation:

Affleck, Willow Georgette. "HOW THE TEACHING AND PRACTICE OF SCIENTIFIC SKETCHING AFFECTS THE QUALITY OF SCIENTIFIC OBSERVATIONS BY HIGH SCHOOL STUDENTS." PhD diss., MONTANA STATE UNIVERSITY Bozeman, 2022.

[107] Consider the role of predictive A.I. in understanding the way proteins work:

Callaway, Ewen. "'It will change everything': DeepMind's A.I. makes gigantic leap in solving protein structures." Nature 588, no. 7837 (2020): 203-205.

[108] Dougherty, Dale. "The maker mindset." In Design, make, play, pp. 25-29. Routledge, 2013.

[109] Lakoff, George, and Mark Johnson. "Conceptual metaphor in everyday language." The journal of Philosophy 77, no. 8 (1980): 453-486.

[110] Swint, Kerwin. "Adams vs. Jefferson: The Birth of Negative Campaigning in the U.S." Mental Floss, 9 Sept. 2012, https://www.mentalfloss.com/article/12487/adams-vs-jefferson-birth-negative-campaigning-us.

[111] Erickson, Emily. "Spanish-American War and the Press." In Encyclopedia of American Journalism, edited by Stephen Vaughn, Routledge, 2011.

[112] Here's a great exploration of the role of authenticity within DBQs. Grant, S. G., Jill M. Gradwell, and Sandra K. Cimbricz. "A QUESTION OF AUTHENTICITY: THE DOCUMENT-BASED QUESTION AS AN ASSESSMENT OF STUDENTS'KNOWLEDGE OF HISTORY." Journal of Curriculum & Supervision 19, no. 4 (2004).

[113] Lipinski, Jed. "The Legend of The Oregon Trail." mental_floss, July 29, 2013. Accessed September 20, 2023. https://www.mentalfloss.com/article/52137/legend-oregon-trail.

[114] Rantala, Jukka, Marika Manninen, and Marko Van den Berg. "Stepping into other people's shoes proves to be a difficult task for high school students: assessing historical empathy through simulation exercise." Journal of Curriculum Studies 48, no. 3 (2016): 323-345.

[115] Vincent, James. "An A.I.-generated artwork's state fair victory fuels arguments over 'what art is' / 'I'm not going to apologize for it,' said the man who submitted the piece." The Verge, September 1, 2022, 9:23 AM PDT. https://www.theverge.com/2022/9/1/23332684/ai-generated-artwork-wins-state-fair-competition-colorado.

[116] Levine, Gloria. "Artists Are Getting Concerned about A.I. Art." 80.lv, 19 September 2022, https://80.lv/articles/artists-are-getting-concerned-about-ai-art/.

[117] Halperin, Julia, and Brian Boucher. "Jeff Koons Radically Downsizes His Studio, Laying off Half His Painting Staff." Artnet, 20 June 2017, https://news.artnet.com/art-world/jeff-koons-radically-downsizes-his-studio-laying-off-half-his-painting-staff-998666.

[118] Artnet News. (2021, July 30). Damien Hirst Laid Off 63 Studio Staffers While Benefiting From a $21 Million Government Bailout Last Fall. Retrieved

from https://news.artnet.com/art-world/damien-hirst-lays-off-63-staffers-2002039

[119] Postman, N. (1982). The disappearance of childhood. Delacorte Press.

[120] It is vital that we recognize that the information and advice provided by an A.I. system is not intended to replace the guidance, expertise, and support of a professional counselor or therapist. If you or someone you know is in need of professional help, please consult a qualified counselor, therapist, or other mental health professional to address your specific concerns and needs. Use of an A.I. system is at your own risk and should not be considered a substitute for professional advice or services. It's also critical to recognize that you are likely a mandatory reporter and if a student is in crisis, you need to follow policies and laws relating to mandatory reporting.

[121] https://spencerauthor.com/dr-alec-couros-on-redefining-information-literacy-in-an-era-of-ai/

[122] Her name is changed here by request. Sadly, a project that benefits refugees in her community turned contentious based on a group of far-right activists.

[123] Csikszentmihalyi, Mihaly. (1990). Flow: The psychology of optimal experience. Harper & Row.

[124] Csikszentmihalyi, Mihaly. (1997). Finding Flow: The Psychology Of Engagement With Everyday Life. New York: BasicBooks.

[125] The White House. "The Impact of Artificial Intelligence on the Future." Whitehouse.gov, December 5, 2022. https://www.whitehouse.gov/uploads/2022/12/The-Impact-of-Artificial-Intelligence-on-the-Future.pdf.

[126] Giang, Vivian. "You Should Plan On Switching Jobs Every Three Years For The Rest Of Your Life." Fast Company. January 7, 2016. https://www.fastcompany.com/3055035/you-should-plan-on-switching-jobs-every-three-years-for-the-rest-of-your-.

[127] Epstein, David. Range: Why Generalists Triumph in a Specialized World. Penguin Publishing Group, 2021.

DR. JOHN SPENCER

Dr. John Spencer is a former middle school teacher and current college professor who focuses on student-centered learning in a changing world. He regularly explores research, interviews educators, deconstructs systems, and studies real-world examples of student empowerment in action. He shares these insights in books, blog posts, journal articles, free resources, animated videos, and podcasts.

He is the co-author of the bestselling books *Launch* and *Empower*. In 2013, he spoke at the White House, sharing a vision for how to empower students to be future-ready through creativity and design thinking. Spencer has led workshops and delivered keynotes around the world with a focus on student creativity and self-direction. He frequently works with schools, districts, and organizations on how to design student-centered learning in blended, hybrid, and remote learning environments.

Email: john@spencerauthor.com
Website: spencerauthor.com
Twitter: @spencerideas
YouTube: spencervideos.com
Instagram: @spencereducation

LOOKING FOR MORE?

Lately, I have been leading sessions, keynotes, and workshops focused on authentic learning in an age of A.I. I use humor and storytelling along with practical strategies to inspire and equip educators at the K-12 and Higher Education levels. If you reach out, we can create something customized for your school, district, or institution.

KEYNOTES

How Will We Respond to the A.I. Revolution?

The A.I. Revolution is here. For some, it's exciting. For others, it feels terrifying. Still others feel baffled and confused by it. Many of us feel a mix of all three emotions. But one thing is clear. It's here and it's not going away. In this keynote, we explore how we might adapt and change as we navigate the new terrain of an A.I.world. We explore the human skills students will need in a world of smart machines. Ultimately, we'll be reminded of the hope and humanity we continue to have in a time of epic change.

Navigating the Maze

We at the beginning of the A.I.revolution and we can't predict what this maze will look like. In this keynote, we explore what vital skills students will need to become self-directed learners who can thrive in the maze. We'll examine how creativity and curiosity can help develop the adaptability students will need as they navigate a complex and unpredictable world fueled by generative A.I.

This is the Future of Education

For all the talk of gadgets and apps, the future of education won't center around a new content delivery system. The future is in your classroom. It's with your students. Your school is packed with creative potential. In this keynote, we tackle what the future of education will look like as we shift toward creativity and innovation in a world of smart machines.

Vintage Innovation

 The best way to prepare students for the future is to empower them in the present. In this keynote or workshop, we explore what it means to use vintage ideas, tools, and strategies in new and relevant ways. Here, we focus on innovation as a focus on "what is best" rather than "what is next." Our focus is on how we move forward in a world of smart machines.

WORKSHOPS

How Will We Respond to the A.I. Revolution?

The A.I. Revolution is here. For some, it's exciting. For others, it feels terrifying. Still others feel baffled and confused by it. Many of us feel a mix of all three emotions. But one thing is clear. It's here and it's not going away. In this workshop, we explore how we might adapt and change as we navigate the new terrain of an A.I.world. We explore the human skills students will need in a world of smart machines. Ultimately, we'll be reminded of the hope and humanity we continue to have in a time of epic change.

A.I. For Personalized Learning

While many companies promise a personalized learning experience focused on adaptive learning (students sitting at a computer getting leveled worksheets), authentic personalized learning is centered on the person. In this workshop, we explore how we can design personalized learning with scaffolds, supports, and differentiation using A.I. We'll explore how we can design something that is human-centered but A.I.-informed.

Integrating A.I. Into PBL

PBL can seem daunting when you have time constraints, standards, and a curriculum map. What does it look like? How do you even get started? In this workshop, we begin with the "why" and move into the "how." As a group, we will do a mini-project and plan out an initial PBL unit. Unlike traditional PBL training, we will explore how we might use generative A.I. into the entire project process.

Printed in the USA
CPSIA information can be obtained
at www.ICGtesting.com
LVHW011820270923
759296LV00020B/85